WHAT PEOPLE F

"Bryan Koch and Daniel McN... g.... nave exposed one of the greatest needs in ministry today. When Jesus said to Nicodemus, "You must be born again," the first marching orders that follow that commitment remain the ultimate marching orders. When Jesus said "Come, follow me," he set in motion a commandment, not a suggestion. In the book *Follow*, the 7 steps to achieve that command are carefully and thoughtfully laid out, that will be the steps to discipleship, preparing one ultimately to lead. One who cannot follow can never lead. Between the statements of Christ, "Come, follow me" and "Well done, thou good and faithful servant," is the blueprint for successful Christian living. A must read." —**Dave Roever**, D.D., Evangelist, Vietnam Veteran, Purple Heart Recipient.

"*Follow: Learning to Follow Jesus* is counter cultural. It stands in contrast to the admonitions, challenges, degree programs and preoccupation that our society has regarding leadership. It states boldly and clearly again and again that true relationship with God and service for God can only be found in being formed in the image of God ... and that only occurs by following Jesus. Bryan and Daniel offer a comprehensive guide not only for the committed follower of Jesus but also for the mentor. *Follow* is not only a must read, it is a must do!"—**Rev. Joseph S. Batluck, Sr.**, D.Min., Chaplain (COL) U.S. Army-Ret, President/Executive Director Teen Challenge Training Center, Inc., Rehrersburg, PA.

"It has been my privilege, for over 20 years, to witness firsthand the passion that Bryan carries for people to become fully devoted followers of Jesus Christ. Whether it is from the pulpit, in small groups, one-on-one, or in pouring into his three sons, a fire burns in Bryan's heart to see people go deep in their walk with Jesus. Now through *Follow*, people around the world will be equipped and challenged to be true followers of our Lord and Savior!"—**Greg Hubbard**, Evangelist.

"*Follow* is the book you have been looking for! Daniel McNaughton and Bryan Koch have written a powerful tool to help you grow in your faith journey. *Follow* presents an intentional process that is amazingly relational and thoroughly biblical. The Spiritual Coaching section is an invaluable discipleship guide that will help you coach others as they learn to follow Jesus!"—**Tom Rees**, Director of Church Planting and Development, PennDel Ministry Network.

"I've always felt like there was a lack of resources to help new believers take their first steps following Christ. Daniel McNaughton fills the gap with Learning to Follow Jesus. It will point new believers in the right direction." —**Mark Batterson**, New York Times Bestselling Author and Lead Pastor of National Community Church (markbatterson.com).

"We are living in a time of mass non-discipleship in the church and it is seriously damaging our witness to Jesus and his cause: In this situation the recovery of discipleship takes on strategic significance. Daniel has blessed us with a fine tool to help get us back on track...we are thankful." —**Alan Hirsch**, author of *The Forgotten Ways* and co-author of *Untamed* and *reJesus* (theforgottenways.org).

"*Learning to Follow Jesus* is thoroughly biblical, practical in its approach, relationally sensitive, and written for the new believer. It incorporates an approach that recognizes the vital role of the Holy Spirit speaking through the Word of God. It can also serve as a tool for influencers who provide healthy relationships for the person learning to be a true follower of Jesus. The simple approach and conversational tone of this excellent volume provides a wonderful resource for those who have embarked on their spiritual journey to follow the Lord as well as for those desiring to share Jesus with others in a mentoring/coaching relationship." —**Dr. Stephen R. Tourville**, Superintendent, PennDel Ministry Network (penndel.org).

"Dr. Daniel McNaughton has written an outstanding tool to enhance the spiritual journey of any earnest Christian pilgrim. With a mixture of personal anecdotes and practical applications, he builds clear and practical steps toward Christian maturity. I commend this book to you with highest recommendation."—**Dr. Don Meyer**, President, University of Valley Forge, Phoenixville, PA (valleyforge.edu).

FOLLOW

• • •

LEARNING TO FOLLOW JESUS

SECOND EDITION

FOLLOW

• • •

LEARNING TO FOLLOW JESUS

BRYAN KOCH
DANIEL McNAUGHTON

LEARNINGTOFOLLOW.NET

MORNING JOY MEDIA

SPRING CITY, PENNSYLVANIA

Published by Morning Joy Media.

Visit morningjoymedia.com for more information on bulk discounts and special promotions, or e-mail your questions to info@morningjoymedia.com.

Cover Design: Staci Focht
Bryan Koch's Photo: Betsy Fick, Mountain Gap Photography
Daniel McNaughton's Photo: Amy Nielsen
Interior Design: Debbie Capeci

Subject Headings:

1. Discipling (Christianity) 2. Spiritual formation. 3. Christian life.

ISBN 978-1-937107-56-7 (paperback)

ISBN 978-1-937107-58-1 (ebook)

Printed in the United States of America

To the memory of my dear wife, Lynn, who was my companion
on this adventurous journey of following Jesus.

—BRYAN KOCH

To my sister, Maralyn Mathias.
Her life, love, and thirst for God inspired me to follow Jesus.

—DANIEL MCNAUGHTON

CONTENTS

ACKNOWLEDGEMENTS

THIS BOOK NEVER WOULD HAVE HAPPENED without the challenge of the strategic planning team at Spring Valley Community Church (SVCC) (Barry Behnke, Lee Bilotta, Jonathan Capeci, Dick Gruber, and Joe Terreri). We were prayerfully dreaming about what we thought God wanted us to do in the following year, and we realized we needed a discipleship tool that would help us learn how to walk with people who were learning to follow Jesus. Someone in that group pointed a finger at me (it felt like the finger of God) and said, "You know you are supposed to write it." They laid hands on me, prayed over me, and helped me adjust my schedule to make time to write it. It was a slow process but eventually *Learning to Follow Jesus* became part of the plan for a discipleship "full court press" at SVCC. We preached a seven-month series (approximately one attribute per month) in the adult, youth, and children's services, discussed and applied the principles weekly in small groups, read and prayed through *Learning to Follow Jesus* in our quiet times, and provided spiritual coaches for many. It was foundational for who we became as a church. So many people at SVCC were part of the process but two have to be mentioned. First, Debbie Capeci of Morning Joy Media graciously joined the vision to publish the Spring Valley version with only a promise that if we ever made profit, we would pay her first. She has been the publisher of all of the contextualized versions of this book except one, which could not be completed because of language and foreign country challenges. I absolutely could not have fulfilled the Learning to Follow vision without her expertise. Second, my wife, Amy, carefully read, reread, and edited various versions of the book. Her insights were invaluable, and her friendship keeps me going. I can't imagine life without her love and support. She has impacted the quality of the writing immeasurably.

About a year after I wrote the first version of this book, I felt the Lord nudging me that people want to be discipled by someone they know. He showed me how to contextualize the book, allowing leaders to replace my stories with theirs so they could have a personalized discipleship tool for the people they influence.

One of the co-authored versions was with my friend Bryan Koch, Lead Pastor of Glad Tidings, Reading, Pennsylvania. It became the "national" version of the book and appears on Amazon and in other public places. It became our national version because the GT Team (Staci Focht, Karen Troutman, Christine Kreisher) produced the whole package of resources, taking the *Follow* vision to the next level. Since then, it has been my sacred privilege to join eleven others as they contextualized the book for their audiences: Trinity Jordan (Elevation Church/Mormons), Bryan Koch (Spanish), Claude Valdes (Word of Life/Youth and Adult), Jeff Leake (Allison Park/Reach Northeast), Sam Masteller (Freedom Life Network), Ron Heitman (Evangel Church), Jon Wegner (Marlton AG), Konan Stephens (C3 Church), Rocco DiTrolio (Argentina/Spanish), Jane Abbate (Women), and Shane Wilson (Christian Life Assembly). We learned something about discipleship from each leader and tried to pass that along to the next version where possible. No two versions are exactly the same.

The second edition of *Follow* with Bryan Koch came about because we realized God is writing a second edition of Bryan's story through the circumstances and challenges surrounding his motorcycle accident. The stories of God's faithfulness and comfort through Bryan's life must be told. We believe they will help many people on their journey to learn to follow Jesus. I am humbled to be on the journey with him as we both seek to honor and serve Jesus with every ounce of our being.

—DANIEL MCNAUGHTON

(Bryan) want to first thank the One that each of us as believers is following and that is Jesus Christ, the Son of God and our Savior. To him be all the glory and honor! Everything written in this book is about and for Jesus, and for those who love him.

There are many people I need to thank for their involvement in this project and I would like to start with my co-author, Dr. Daniel McNaughton, who carried the vision and passion for *Learning to Follow Jesus* and invited me to be a part of it. Debbie Capeci, thank you for all your expertise in this project. May Morning Joy Media be blessed in every way as you help writers bring their heart to print.

Lynn, my lovely wife and lifelong friend, who served Jesus since the time she was a little girl until she went home to be with him, has taught me more about loving Christ than anyone else I know. To my boys, Ben, Bryce, and Brett, my daugthers-in-law and my grandson Jackson, you inspire me to continue to keep following Jesus. To my sister-in-law Ronda and her husband David, thank you for sharing your story of healing to encourage the faith of others.

I am grateful for my father and mother, Ted and Donna Koch. My parents have been so encouraging and incredibly supportive in every conceivable way my entire life. No one could ever ask for greater parents. My sister is a fully devoted follower who maximizes her influence and freely shares her love. Marsha, you're the best!

I certainly want to thank the GT leadership team, our staff and executive board for their belief in me, as well as their practical and passionate support. Karen Troutman, thank you for your oversight of this project, as well as all the helpful suggestions through each step of its completion. I know we are not supposed to judge a book by its cover, but we often do, so Staci Focht thank you for your artistry and graphic design.

Jim and Marijo Smith, what can I say? Thank you for the hours upon hours of editing, encouraging, and coaching. You have really helped me begin to find my voice on paper in addition to in the pulpit, but your friendship has been the greatest blessing.

Finally, to my church family I want to say thank you for allowing me the privilege of being a part of the ministry of Glad Tidings Assembly of God over these twenty-plus years. My prayer is that this book will help deepen your understanding of the love that God has for you! May God be praised!

—BRYAN KOCH

INTRODUCTION

I (Daniel) WILL NEVER FORGET sitting in my office at a church in Toronto, Ontario, where I served as an assistant pastor when it dawned on me that I had never been systematically and intentionally shown how to become a disciple, a fully-devoted follower of Jesus. It was shocking to realize the irony. I was raised in a Christian home, attended many Christian meetings, graduated from a denominational college with a degree in Bible, received a masters degree from a reputable seminary, completed more than half of my Ph.D. in Biblical Studies, and was serving as a pastor, but I was never shown how to systematically disciple people. I had invited Christ into my life and was attempting to follow Jesus to the best of my ability, but it was fuzzy. What is a disciple? What does a disciple look like? What does a disciple do?

This was especially disturbing to me because the Gospel of Matthew concludes with the resurrected Jesus appearing to his followers giving them only one command in the Great Commission. It is not "go" as I had often heard preached. It is "make disciples." One command! Why was it fuzzy?

Over the past eighteen years, I have asked many of my friends if they can clearly and succinctly describe what a disciple is and how to make one. Unfortunately, most are like I was…fuzzy. That does not mean we are not making disciples. It is just not clear. Rather than rant about how this could be, I decided to go on a quest to learn how. We cannot change the past, but we can be part of a future that rediscovers what Jesus had in mind when he gave the one command.

This book is designed to be a simple, practical guide for those who want to learn to follow Jesus. There are four main parts to the guide: an overview of the seven essential attributes of the follower of Jesus (also called "First Steps"); a step-by-step development of each attribute; resources to augment each attribute; and spiritual coaching guides. To get the most out of this book, you will need to read the biblical passages, memorize the Scriptures, write out your answers in the book, pray the prayers, and discuss your progress with a spiritual coach. The goal is not simply to complete the book. The goal is that you will be growing in each of the seven attributes for the rest of your life. When you finish working through the guide one time and are growing in each attribute, you are ready to come alongside another person to help him or her learn to follow Jesus. Keep it going! If you help one person a year follow Jesus and if each person you help does the same, and those they help do the same, in thirty-three years we could reach the entire world with the gospel. I want be part of a worldwide movement of people who focus their lives on the "one thing" that matters most to Jesus. How about you?

—DANIEL MCNAUGHTON

LOOKING BACK OVER THE YEARS before I (Bryan) became a pastor, I realized that I received what many Christians never do—personal spiritual coaching. I was one of the youngest players in the Chicago White Sox organization, and an older player named Paul recognized that I was a believer and that I loved the Lord. The way my baseball coach taught me the game at a deeper, professional level, my spiritual coach did the same for my faith. He didn't come up with formal teaching sessions or lessons; instead, we did life together. Paul knew the meaning of following Jesus and of his invitation and promise in Matthew 4:19, "'Come, follow me,' Jesus said, 'and I will make you fishers of men.'"

When we receive an invitation, it means that person wants to be with us. It amazes me that Jesus even invites me. He invites all of us. As equally amazing as the invitation is Jesus' promise to make us like him. Come to me and I will make you a healer. Come to me and I will make you an influence. Come to me and I will teach you to pray. Come to me and I will help you manage. Come to me and I will teach you to love.

Follow is the big idea of the Gospel of Matthew and each attribute that you will learn about comes from this former tax collector and faithful follower as he was inspired by the Holy Spirit. *Follow* is designed to take you back to the cornerstone of our spiritual foundation, which is Jesus. *Follow* is a resource with formal lessons that will guide you in a practical and biblical approach to spiritual coaching and discipleship.

My hope and prayer is that this book will allow you to experience the invitation and promise of coming to Jesus and letting him transform you into a fully devoted follower.

— BRYAN KOCH

CREED

FOR FOLLOWERS OF JESUS CHRIST

I have decided to follow Jesus. I believe that he is God in the flesh, and I have received him as my personal Lord and Savior. Having entered into a restored relationship with my Heavenly Father, the Creator himself, I will commit to spending time with him daily. I will listen carefully for his voice each day, as I allow him to use me as a conduit of healing for others. I will pay attention to how the Holy Spirit will direct me to influence others towards Jesus, and I will make loving God and loving others my highest priorities. I commit to growing in continual communication with the Father through prayer, and I give permission to the Holy Spirit to direct me in how I manage my time, my talent, and my treasure. In doing these things, I choose to seek God and his kingdom first, believing that he will provide for the other concerns of my life. I also accept the charge to now give it away, realizing that I am commissioned to make disciples and offer spiritual coaching to others. Choosing to follow Jesus will be my daily decision, and my lifelong pursuit. Choosing to follow Jesus will change everything.

GETTING STARTED

CONGRATULATIONS ON YOUR DECISION to become a follower of Jesus! You may or may not realize it yet, but following Jesus is the most important decision you will ever make in your life. It will affect every future decision you will make on this earth, and it will affect where you spend eternity. You have made a great decision! This book is designed to help you develop in your walk with Christ so you can know and honor God the rest of your life and for eternity.

Since it is such an important decision, it is worthwhile to take a few minutes to review what it means to become a follower of Jesus. John 1:12 describes becoming part of God's family as a two-part decision: "Yet to all who received him [Jesus], to those who believed in his name, he gave the right to become children of God." You must **receive** Christ and **believe** in his name. Even though the Bible teaches that Jesus created the universe (John 1:3), he never forces anyone to follow him. God gives you freedom to accept or reject Jesus. By receiving Jesus, you accept that he was God, that he was the perfect representation of what God is like. By believing in his name, you are trusting that Jesus paid the price for your sin when he died on the cross. John 3:16 says, "For God so loved the world that he gave his one and only Son, that whoever believes in him shall not perish but have eternal life." God came to earth because he loves every one of us and wants us to have eternal life. Jesus describes eternal life this way in John 17:3, "Now this is eternal life: that they may know you, the only true God, and Jesus Christ, whom you have sent." Eternal life is knowing Jesus. If you are uncertain whether or not you have done that, why not take a minute right now and make sure. If you are unaccustomed to praying or if you are unsure what to pray, you can join me in the following prayer.

Prayer:

Dear Heavenly Father, I want to become a follower of Jesus. I receive Jesus into my life. I believe he was God and that he came to pay the price for my sin when he died on the cross. Please forgive me for living life my own way. I turn away from that life and I turn toward you. As best I know how and with your help, I want to live for you from this day forward. Amen.

Having received Jesus and believed what he came to do, you can now be certain that you are part of God's family.

There are a few things that are important to keep in mind from the beginning. First, becoming a follower of Jesus is not just about learning information. It is much more than that. Jesus said that those who come to him, hear his words, and put them into practice will be the ones who will have a foundation on which to stand when tough times come. Building a solid foundation requires you to bring everything to Christ, hear God's Word, and then put it into practice.

Second, most of us learn best from watching and learning from others. In other words, "more is caught than is taught." That's why we encourage you to put yourself in four contexts where you can learn from others: a large gathering where you can worship God and hear Bible teaching (a church service); a small group where you can apply the Bible to your life and live out your faith with others; a one-on-one mentoring meeting with a spiritual coach; and a private time with God on your own. *Follow* is a tool that can help you develop in your private time with God and can serve as a discussion starter with you and your coach. We all need people with whom we can share our honest thoughts, our successes, our failures, and our questions, especially when we are just starting out on a new venture. A spiritual coach and the people in your small group will help you learn how to honor God in every area of life. They will probably not have all the answers to your questions, but they may serve as resources to you, and they are committed to sharing what they know with you.

What church do you plan to attend? ....

Would you like a spiritual coach? ....

Would you like more information about small groups? ...

If you don't have a spiritual coach or a small group yet, please contact a pastor to help you find both.

Third, following Christ is a process. You will not be perfect, nor will your spiritual coach or the members of your small group. Only Jesus is perfect. When you follow Christ, you accept what he has done for you. Knowing that your eternal destiny depends on Jesus' righteousness and not yours will set you free from trying to work to get God to love you. Jesus has already pleased God for you. There is nothing you can ever do to make God love you more. His love for you is limitless and eternal. His thoughts about you are always good. Enjoy your newfound reality of knowing God is pleased with you because of Jesus. Don't try to work to please him. Just live your life in gratitude for his amazing love and acceptance. As you spend time with other followers of Christ and with your loving Heavenly Father, you will discover that you want to become more like Christ, and you will change. God will change you.

This book is designed to help you cultivate good habits that will support a healthy spiritual environment for your new walk with Christ. To get the most out of this tool, you will need to make the following choices:

→ Set aside about fifteen minutes per day to focus on your spiritual growth. Every relationship takes time. Your relationship with Christ is no exception. Choose a time slot that will work consistently for you. Many people find that the morning is best. Others believe the time before they go to bed is best. Some people do both. The most important thing is that you make time for your spiritual growth. You may have to experiment but pick a time that works for you. What time will work best for you on a daily basis?

→ Write your answers in the book. You will retain more of what you are learning if you take the time to write your answers.

→ Read the Bible references for yourself. If you don't have a Bible in a modern translation (New International Version [NIV] and New Living Translation [NLT] are good ones), ask your spiritual coach to help you find one. What translation will you use?

→ Memorize the verses linked with each attribute. Do your best to learn them word-for-word. If you take a little time each day, you will discover they will come to mind much easier. Review all previously memorized verses daily; that puts them into your long-term memory. You won't regret it.

→ Put what you learn into practice right away. A follower of Jesus is one who learns what Jesus is like and then takes action to become like him. Enjoy the journey.

FIRST STEPS

• • •

AN OVERVIEW
OF THE ATTRIBUTES

ATTRIBUTE ONE · OVERVIEW
LEARN TO BE WITH JESUS

Scripture Memory (new):

"Come, follow me," Jesus said, "and I will send you out to fish for people." Matthew 4:19

Read: Matthew 4:18–22

ONE OF THE FIRST THINGS we learn when we become followers of Jesus is he wants us to be with him.

What did Jesus say to Peter and Andrew in Matthew 4:18–22?

Notice that Jesus took the initiative in their relationship. He loved them and he loves you as well. He is and has been reaching out to you from the time you were born. He invites you to follow him—to be with him.

In John's Gospel in chapter 1, we also see Jesus inviting people to be with him. Andrew started following Jesus after John the Baptist said Jesus was "the Lamb of God who takes away the sin of the world." When Jesus saw Andrew following him, he asked, "What do you want?" Andrew responded by calling Jesus "Teacher" and asking where he was staying. Jesus invited him, "Come and see" and they spent the whole day together. There is no higher calling in life than Jesus' call to be with him. You may do great things for him. You may help many people learn to follow him and that's great, but your primary calling is just to be with him.

Does it surprise you that the Creator of the universe invites us to be with him? The psalmist writes, "What is mankind that you are mindful of them, human beings that you care for them?" (Psalm 8:4). God cares about you and wants you to be close to him. How does it make you feel to know that Jesus wants you to be with him? (Pause right now and take a few minutes to thank the Lord for calling you to follow him. Tell him how you feel and affirm your commitment to follow him.)

What are some of your feelings about Jesus' calling you to be one of his followers? ....

....

....

What did Peter, Andrew, James and John have to leave behind to follow Jesus? ....

....

....

What would be tough for you to leave behind to follow him? ....

....

While it may seem tough to leave something behind right now, you will soon realize that nothing you leave behind can compare in value to the amazing gift that you have as a follower of Jesus.

In Matthew 13:44–46 Jesus compares finding the kingdom of God (having Christ rule in your heart) to a man who found a treasure in a field. He hid the treasure and then in his great joy went and sold all he had and bought that field. He also compared it to a merchant who found a pearl of great value and went away and sold everything he had and bought it. Nothing you have can compare with the treasure you have when you follow Jesus.

One of the best parts about following Jesus is that he will never leave you. The last words in the book of Matthew say this, "And surely I am with you always, to the very end of the age." Jesus' commitment to be with you is a forever thing. Though others leave you or don't fulfill their commitments to you, Jesus promises that he will always be with you both now and throughout eternity. You will never be alone again.

What did Jesus say would happen if Peter and Andrew followed him?

Following Jesus will change your life. He promised to transform his disciples from being fishermen who could catch fish to fishermen who would catch people. He will transform your life as well so you can become the person he designed you to be. You may not know what that is just yet, but it will become clear as you follow him. There is one thing you can be sure of, however: Jesus will lead you to make a difference in the lives of others. That was his purpose for coming, and it was the one thing he told his disciples to do as he was leaving. Don't let that intimidate you. It will be a wonderful and fulfilling journey. He will show you the next steps, and he will always be with you. Just enjoy being with him now.

Prayer:

Heavenly Father, thank you for inviting me to follow you. It amazes me that you care about me enough to want to be with me. I respond to your invitation again and declare that I am your follower. I will joyfully leave behind the things you ask me to because I believe that I will be better off with you. Change me into the person you want me to become. I rest in your commitment to be with me forever. I also rest in your presence right now, my heart's true home. Amen.

ATTRIBUTE TWO · OVERVIEW
LEARN TO LISTEN

Scripture Memory:

"Come, _____ me," Jesus _____, "and I will send you _____ to _____ for people." Matthew ____:19

"Come, follow me," Jesus said, "and I will send you out to fish for people." Matthew 4:19

Read: Matthew 4:23–25

JESUS BEGAN TEACHING his followers by inviting them to observe what he was doing. According to these verses, what did the first followers of Jesus observe him doing? ....

As a follower of Jesus, it is important for you to observe Jesus' teaching, preaching, and healing as well. (We'll talk about Jesus' healing in the next attribute.) You will find a summary of Jesus' preaching in Matthew 4:17: "From that time on Jesus began to preach, 'Repent, for the kingdom of heaven has come near.'" There are a couple of terms that need defining. First, the word "repent" means "to turn away from something and to turn toward something else." When some people hear the word "repent" they think of it negatively. Perhaps it stirs up an image of a screaming evangelist. Repentance, however, is positive. When we repent we get to turn away from the things that are keeping us from following

Christ, and then turn to him, the Author of life.

Second, "the kingdom of heaven" means that God can have first place in your heart. I don't know what comes to your mind when you think of "kingdom," but I think of walled cities, castles and kings, like the Battle of Helms Deep in the movie *Lord of the Rings: The Two Towers*. The kingdom of heaven is different from that. God's kingdom is not about weapons and war machines, but there is a king. Luke 17:20b–21 states, "The coming of the kingdom of God is not something that can be observed, nor will people say, 'Here it is,' or 'There it is,' because the kingdom of God is in your midst." When the kingdom of God comes in your life, he rules your heart. Your life will change, not by force but by the power of God. We can change because Jesus is near to help us and empower us. That's great news.

Matthew 4:23 describes Jesus' preaching about the kingdom like that. The fact that we can turn away from our old lives and have God rule in our hearts is great news. But it's not without a cost. Your priorities will change as you make room for God to rule in your life. You know what rules your heart by where you give your treasures: your time, your talent, and your money.

What would you say are the top priorities in your life right now?

What are some things you need to turn away from (repent) so that Christ can rule in your heart?

Repentance is ongoing for a follower of Christ. No one will ever be perfect except Jesus. As you get to know Jesus better, repentance will become easier because you will realize that his ways are always best!

What good things could happen if you were to repent from these things?

20

What are some things from which you would like to repent?

I want to repent from: I can turn from this and to God by:

1. ....

2. ....

3. ....

You may want to share these with your spiritual coach, who can encourage you in your decisions. Your spiritual coach is going through the same process, so you don't need to worry about what he or she will think of you. Romans 3:23 reminds us that "All have sinned and fall short of the glory of God." There's another great passage about this as well in 1 John 1:8–10:

> If we claim to be without sin, we deceive ourselves and the truth is not in us. If we confess our sins, he is faithful and just and will forgive us our sins and purify us from all unrighteousness. If we claim we have not sinned, we make him out to be a liar and his word is not in us.

Repentance just brings these things to light so we can deal with them, with God's help. Remember, he is with you.

Prayer:

Dear Jesus, thank you for the invitation to turn away from my old life. I do actively turn away from the things I have done that are wrong and I turn to you. I repent from [tell God the things you mentioned previously]. Thank you for replacing those things with your leadership in my life. I welcome you into my life. Thank you also for inviting me to bring my pain to you. Please bring healing to my life in every way. I am so grateful to you for helping me find life in you, Jesus Christ. Amen.

ATTRIBUTE THREE · OVERVIEW
LEARN TO HEAL

Scripture Memory:
"_____ , follow _____ ," Jesus said, "_____ I will _____
you out to fish for _____ ." Matthew ___ : ____

"Come, follow me," Jesus said, "and I will send you out to fish for people." Matthew 4:19

Read: Matthew 4:23–25

As I was looking at Jesus' method for helping people learn to follow him, it struck me that one of the first things he did was invite his followers to be with him while he preached and healed people. There is nothing like seeing God heal firsthand. Based on these verses, what kinds of things did Jesus heal?[1]

During the summer of 1982, I (Bryan) was blessed to live my lifelong dream of being a professional baseball player when I was drafted by the Chicago White Sox and joined their farm system. Those years would become some of the most exciting times of my life. After three years of enjoying the culture of minor league baseball, the cheers of the crowd ended when a fastball hit me in the left eye. As I fell across home plate attempting to regain my senses, little did I know that this injury would end my career and dreams of being a big league player. After consulting several doctors, I learned

22

that I had not only lost my career, but also about seventy-five percent of my vision in that eye.

A lifetime of vision problems became worse in the summer of 2006 when I awoke with irritation and pain in my right eye—the good one. Thinking it was a minor problem, I scheduled an appointment with my eye doctor only to find out that the irritation was caused by my contact lens tearing a hole in the very center of my cornea. My doctor was concerned that even if the hole in my cornea healed, the remaining scar tissue could still impair my vision. Coupled with the injury to my left eye, the prognosis was grim. My family and my congregation began to pray and intercede for my healing and that is exactly what happened. Jesus Christ healed and restored my right eye. Not only did Jesus heal the hole in my cornea, but he also removed all traces of scar tissue, to my doctor's amazement.

Up until June of 2015, I thought that losing the sight in my left eye was my story. But God wrote a new chapter on June 7. After church, my wife, Lynn, and I went for a motorcycle ride, something that we had done hundreds of times before. But on that day, about one mile from our home, we were hit head-on by a drunk driver. The impact of the crash caused Lynn to lose her life and me to lose my left leg. I was flown by helicopter to the Reading Hospital where my prognosis was grim. But God did in my life what he had done before. He brought miraculous healing to my body. We serve a God of miracles, and I have experienced this personally, not once, but twice in my lifetime.

When I (Daniel) was about five years old, I also experienced a dramatic healing. I was trying to get some glue in a high cabinet in our home by using the drawers below as steps. When my foot slipped, I hung my arm inside one of the drawers and broke a bone around my elbow. As we were scurrying around to go to the hospital, Nina Gaddis, a guest speaker who was staying at our home, prayed for my arm and God healed it. I'll never forget her quietly asking God to heal my arm while she lightly touched it. As she prayed, my arm immediately stopped hurting and returned to a normal appearance. That experience shaped how I think about God's miraculous intervention.

Fast-forward to the second year of my doctoral program (1987–1988) at the University of Toronto. I took a class entitled, "Synoptic Miracles." The professor began that course by making a statement similar to the following:

> No one in the twentieth century with a thinking mind could possibly believe in a virgin birth, miracles, or the bodily resurrection. We know these things don't happen. So when we read the miracle stories of the Bible, we are not talking about what happened. We are reading perhaps what they thought happened but not what actually happened.

Based on that assumption, he proceeded to explain how we need to demythologize the stories of Jesus to get to the real, historical Jesus. I remember walking through this thought process: "I'm definitely in the twentieth century. I believe I have a thinking mind. I am engaged fully in the academic process and excelling. And, I not only believe in miracles, I have experienced them." I understand skepticism. I have my own struggles with it, but I had never encountered someone who said it just couldn't have happened. Needless to say, that was a fascinating semester for the both of us. I challenged his worldview and he challenged mine. I'll share more of my journey about that in the following pages.

As you begin to follow Jesus, be open to God's supernatural intervention in your life. Talk with God throughout your day with words of love, praise, and need. It's not about the formality of your prayer, but the sincerity of your heart. Just ask God to do the miraculous, place your faith in him, and see what happens.

While you are pondering that thought, consider that there are eighty-eight references in the New Testament to healing. Some of them are stories of Jesus healing someone. Others, however, refer to God healing people through the prayers of his followers (Luke 9:2, 9:6; Acts 3:16, 4:9–30, 5:16, 8:7, 9:34, 10:38, 14:9, 28:8). In fact, 1 Corinthians 12:9 refers to "gifts of healing" being given to some of Christ's followers. You need to know that since Christ lives in you, he can provide healing through you. Begin to pray and ask him to meet needs about which you are aware.

We all need healing. You may need physical or emotional healing. You might need healing in a relationship. We all need spiritual healing. Whatever your need, you can bring it to the Lord and ask him. I wish I understood why God chooses to heal sometimes and not others, but I do not. But you never want it to be said about you that you could have had healing but you didn't ask. So ask and trust God.

What kinds of things do you need healing for today?

....

....

Share these with your spiritual coach, who will agree with you in prayer for your healing.

Prayer:

Thank you, Heavenly Father, for reminding me that you care about the details of my life. I praise you and thank you for the new life you are giving me through Jesus. In response to what I am reading today, I ask you for healing for [name the areas for which you want healing]. (Describe how the problem has caused you pain or suffering. Tell it to God even though he already knows.) Your Word tells me that you are compassionate toward me and that you care about me. I ask that you would have mercy on me about [name the area]. I trust that you love me and care about me. Thank you for your kindness to me. In Jesus' name I pray, amen.

ATTRIBUTE FOUR · OVERVIEW
LEARN TO INFLUENCE

Scripture Memory:

"Come, _____ _____," Jesus said, " _____ __ _____
_____ you __ to __ for people." _____ __:__

*"Come, follow me," Jesus said, "and I will send you out to fish
for people." Matthew 4:19*

Read: Matthew 5:13–16

WHO ARE YOU? And why are you here? Many people spend
their whole lives not ever knowing why they are on the
planet. At the beginning of his teaching Jesus clearly defines
who we are as his followers.

What two metaphors does Jesus use to describe his
followers?

Both of these metaphors describe our identity as
influencers for God. Salt preserves things and makes our
food taste better. When it comes in contact with something it has an effect. Light helps us see things more clearly,
especially when it is dark. The reason we are on this planet is
to impact people for God. We are not here for ourselves. As
Rick Warren so aptly puts it:

> It's not about you. The purpose of your life is far greater than
> your own personal fulfillment, your peace of mind, or even
> your happiness. It's far greater than your family, your career, or

even your wildest dreams and ambitions. If you want to know why you were placed on this planet, you must start with God. You were born *by* his purpose and *for* his purpose.[1]

The ultimate goal for everything you do is to influence people for God so they might also praise God in heaven. You are an attractor for God.

This thought could be a bit overwhelming. You might say, "How can I ever attract people to God? My life is not perfect enough to point people to God." The answer? God will attract people to himself through your life as you continue to learn to follow him. Of course you are not perfect, but he is. As God begins to change you, people will notice and they may want to know how that happened.

Have you ever noticed that when you hang out with someone you become like them? Do you have a friend with whom you share special vocabulary or a favorite handshake or similar jokes? The same will become true with you and Jesus. As you are with him, you will start to become more and more like him. For most of us, this is such a gradual process that we may not even see it, but others will. And when they do, we are living up to our identity as salt and light.

Make a list of friends, family, neighbors, and co-workers who could benefit from becoming followers of Jesus.

....

....

....

....

....

....

....

....

....

....

Prayer:

Heavenly Father, thank you for defining who I am and why I'm on this planet. Life is starting to make sense. I really want you to influence people through my life. Continue to change me so that I reflect you clearly. I know I can't do this on my own and you are not asking me to. I rest in our relationship right now. You are so good. I bring my friends and family to you now. Would you pull them to you? Would you open their eyes to see how empty their lives are without you? Would you help them see their need for a forever relationship with you? Remove any confusion or barriers that would keep them from getting to know you. Help my life to be attractive for you. Give me wisdom to know how to approach these relationships. Help me to love them. I bring them to you. Amen.

ATTRIBUTE FIVE · OVERVIEW
LEARN TO LOVE

Scripture Memory:

"Come, _____ ____," _____ _____, "and I ____ ____
_____ ____ __ ____ ____ ____." _____ ____ : ____

---

*"Come, follow me," Jesus said, "and I will send you out to fish
for people." Matthew 4:19*

Read: Matthew 5:43–48

FOLLOWERS OF JESUS LEARN from the beginning and all
throughout their lives that love is the foundation for
everything. Many people think that loving God is only a
personal and private thing. While loving God is both personal
and private, it is not only that. Loving God will also lead
you to love people. What two commands does Jesus make in
Matthew 5:44? ....

If you wrote, "love your enemies" and "pray for those
who persecute you," you are correct. According to Matthew
5:45, what does Jesus say will happen if we obey him in
these commands? ....

One thing that identifies an authentic follower of Jesus
is love for others. As you are learning to follow, it may seem
quite foreign to you that you could love people who have

hurt you. If you have people who have caused you pain in your past whom you find difficult to love, I have good news for you. Jesus will enable you to rise above your past hurts. As you get to know Jesus better and as you learn to trust and obey him, you will find great freedom. *Follow* can help you take steps in that direction.[1] You will pour out your heart to God and you will enjoy the kindness and the compassion of God as he heals you.

Today's challenge, however, is actually a decision only you can make. Will you obey Jesus' commands in Matthew 5:43–48 to love your enemies and pray for those who persecute you? As you are thinking about this, I want you to know a couple of things. First, the type of love Jesus is talking about is not a feeling. Love means you do what is best for the other person regardless of how you or they feel about it. It is choosing to see that person as someone Jesus loves. As such, it is a decision. Choosing to love someone who had hurt me would never have happened in my life if Jesus did not teach me to do it. I would never have considered it. It is not logical or normal for me to do good to my enemies. Second, loving someone does not necessarily mean that you do what the other person wants. That would not always be loving. For example, it is not the most loving thing to allow abusive people to continue to abuse you. The most loving thing might be for you to help those people experience the consequences of their actions. Third, the only way you are going to be able to love people the way they need to be loved, especially your enemies, is with Jesus' help. That's why you pray for them. Tell God your honest feelings about those people and what you want to happen to them (good or bad).

As you open up this dialogue with God, a wonderful thing will happen. Your capacity to love God will grow as will your capacity to love people. You will also discover that your responses to people can be independent of their actions and their responses toward you. You may even find yourself starting to feel compassion toward them. You may not like them, but you will be able to love them. I have found great freedom in knowing I do not have to hate my enemies anymore.

Having encouraged you, it is time now to act. For whom do you need to pray? ....

Join with me now as we pray.

Prayer:

Heavenly Father, you are challenging me today to do something that goes against my nature, to love my enemies. I confess I have not done that in the past, but I want to learn from you how to do that. I pray now for [mention the person's name]. [Say his name] became my enemy when he [tell God what the person did to hurt you even though God already knows.] You know how that hurt me and the decisions I made because of that. I bring that to you right now. Continue the healing process in my life. I know that you love [mention the name] and that you want the best for his life. I ask that your plan for him will be accomplished. Help me to act in loving ways toward [name] in the future. Teach me how to love like you love. Amen.

ATTRIBUTE SIX · OVERVIEW
LEARN TO PRAY

Scripture Memory:

" _____ , _____ ," _____ , " _____
_____ _____ _____ _____ _____ ."
_____ _____ : _____

"Come, follow me," Jesus said, "and I will send you out to fish for people." Matthew 4:19

Read: Matthew 6:5–15

JESUS' FOLLOWERS didn't follow him long before they realized that prayer was important and normal for him. Luke 5:16 says this, "But Jesus often withdrew to lonely places and prayed." As a follower of Jesus, it will become normal for you to pray as well. In this passage, Jesus is contrasting good prayer and bad prayer.

What is the difference between good and bad prayer?

....

....

....

In Matthew 6:9–13, Jesus teaches his followers how to pray. The Lord's Prayer is not intended to be a rote prayer that is prayed over and over but rather is an example of how to pray. Think about prayer more as a conversation between two friends, not a formula. You can talk with God about anything. Feel free to use your own words to express your thoughts and concerns to God. Notice the components of this simple prayer:

→ **Relationship**—"Our Father in heaven" teaches us that we are in a loving relationship with our Heavenly Father and with others as well who are part of the family.

→ **Respect**—"Hallowed be your name" teaches us that God is holy and as such must receive honor and respect. Tell the Lord how much he means to you and honor him.

→ **Reign**—"Let your kingdom come" teaches us that we start with what God wants. He wants to rule in our hearts. When we pray "let your kingdom come," we are inviting him be our leader and our guide. We bow our lives before him when we pray, "let your kingdom come."

→ **Food**—"Give us today our daily bread" teaches us that we can ask God to meet our basic needs today. When our lives are lined up with his values, we can ask for fuel to do it.

→ **Forgiveness**—"Forgive us our debts as we also have forgiven our debtors" teaches us that when we pray we remember we need forgiveness as much as everyone else. God expects us to model to others the forgiveness he gives to us. In fact, this is so important for us that God requires us to forgive others in order for us to receive his forgiveness. This is important!

→ **Freedom**—"And lead us not into temptation but deliver us from the evil one" teaches us that God can help us be victorious in every temptation. With God's help we can be delivered from the things that are destroying us.

Where does Jesus say his followers should go when we pray?..

....

It's really important to find a quiet place and a time that you can be alone to pray. There are many ways to do this. You can get up a few minutes earlier than usual, perhaps before others get out of bed. Or, you can go for a walk in the neighborhood.

When and where do you plan to pray?........................

....

You will want to set aside time each day to follow Jesus in prayer. Start with a small amount of time, perhaps five to ten minutes. Eventually, you will probably increase the time but for now set aside at least five minutes. You learn to pray by praying. Feel free to use the six components of the Lord's Prayer to direct your thoughts and words to God. Use your own words to express your thoughts to God. Prayer is not a magic formula. It's just a friend talking with a friend.

As you talk with God, take a few minutes to listen to him as well. Rarely does God speak audibly. In fact, it has never happened to me. But I do have thoughts and impressions that come to me occasionally when I pray, and I have learned that's one of the ways he speaks to me. If you think God might be speaking to you, take a moment to write it down and test it out. One good test is whether it is consistent with what God says elsewhere in his Word. God never contradicts himself. You may not yet know whether what you hear is God or not so feel free to share it with your spiritual coach or a pastor to confirm it. You will learn to tell the difference between what God is speaking and what are just your thoughts.

Prayer:

God, it is great to know I am part of your family and that you are my loving heavenly Father. I give you honor.

Truly there is no one like you. I respect you more than I can adequately express with my own words. Please rule my life. Lead me today. Thank you for your provisions for my life. I have everything I really need. Forgive me where I have done wrong. (Go ahead and mention specific things for which you know you need forgiveness.) I choose to extend your forgiveness to everyone around me as well, Lord, because you have been so gracious to me. Lead me away from doing the things I know are destructive and to a path of freedom today. It's great having you in my life. Amen.

ATTRIBUTE SEVEN • OVERVIEW
LEARN TO MANAGE

"Come, follow me," Jesus said, "and I will send you out to fish for people." Matthew 4:19

Read: Matthew 6:19–24

WHAT WOULD YOU CONSIDER to be your treasure? For some of us, it is definitely our money. For others, it's reputation. Or time off. Or shoes. Really! I (Daniel) have a box of treasures; actually, several stashes of treasures. We have moved that box from place to place—a Punt, Pass and Kick trophy from the second grade, class certificates from the fifth grade, my first athletic letter when I was in seventh grade, some pictures and newspaper clippings of years as a basketball player. Treasures. Stuff! I got into the box not that long ago and realized several of the trophies were broken. The paper clippings are yellowing. They are simply not going to last.

Jesus is kind enough and direct enough to address the issue of what we treasure early in our lives as followers. He wants the best for us, and he can't bear for us to waste time and energy on things that simply aren't part of our trip as a follower.

What kinds of things does Jesus say we should not store up?

What are some examples of things that moths can eat, rust can destroy, and thieves can steal?

What reason does Jesus give for not storing up these things?

What kinds of things does Jesus say we should store up?

What reason does Jesus give for storing up these things?

You must not miss Jesus' statement, "For where your treasure is, there your heart will be also." He does *not* say as many think, "For where your heart is, there your treasure will be also." He says the opposite. In other words, where you put your treasure, that's where your heart will go. Your treasures really are your time, your talent, and your money. He's saying that where you choose to invest your treasure, you will discover your heart will follow. Your heart is submissive to your treasure. He says it blatantly in verse 24, "You cannot serve both God and money." It's impossible to love both. You have to make a choice.

This was a tough one for me early in my walk with Christ. We always had lots of food on the table and adequate clothing, but I grew up thinking that I needed and wanted to have a lot more. It became somewhat of an obsession. I wanted to be wealthy. Although my father was a minister, I didn't even consider being a minister because I was convinced I could not make the kind of money I wanted. I had to surrender my desire to make lots of money when I became a follower of Jesus. You will, too. It's one of the best decisions I have ever made. God supplies everything I need. I am certain I have also enjoyed the resources he has given me far more than if I had not surrendered. I am confident you will too. And it all makes sense based on what we have already learned as a follower. We exist for him and we fulfill our purpose in this life when we use his resources to join what he is doing in the world. The psalmist says it this way in Psalm 24:1, "The earth is the LORD's, and everything in it." That's another way of saying, "It's all God's."

What kinds of things do you treasure that you need to surrender to God?

What are some places or areas of your life in which you need to invest so that your heart goes where you want it to go?

What are you going to invest in each of these areas?

Share your decisions with your spiritual coach this week. Ask your spiritual coach how she invests her treasures (time, talent, and money) so that her heart lines up with God's purposes in the world. Also, ask her what has happened as a result of these investments.

Prayer:

Jesus, thank you for telling me the truth about my treasures. I choose to serve you and not money. Help me to be courageous enough to invest in things that I know will matter to you. Help me to stop investing in things that won't matter one second after I pass from this life. I give this whole area of treasures over to you. I trust you with my life and my treasure. Amen.

ATTRIBUTE ONE

• • •

LEARN TO BE WITH JESUS

ATTRIBUTE ONE
INTRODUCTION
LEARN TO BE WITH JESUS

THE MORE TIME YOU SPEND WITH JESUS, the more you will love him and become like him. That's why it is so important to learn how to be with him.

When you first get married, a lot of your life changes as you learn how to be with the other person. Everything is affected—how you do things, when you do things, everything. As a follower of Jesus, you are learning how to make Jesus your first priority. Before you may have just done things without thinking much of him, but now that you realize he is always with you, you may start to view things or do things differently. You are learning to allow him to lead in every area of life and to show you life from his perspective. In this lesson we are going to focus on learning how to enjoy being with him throughout the day regardless of what else is going on.

A logical time to be with him is during a quiet time. We'll talk a little about how to set that up. A quiet devotional time is a good start, but Jesus is with you *always*. As you learn to remain in him, to be with him, he will change everything. He'll show you how to live life to the full in a way that brings God honor. He'll teach you through his Word and in your prayer time how to hear his voice. He'll even show you how to love people and to live a joyful life. Sound good? It is! Serving Jesus is the best life! That's what this lesson is about.

ATTRIBUTE ONE · STEP ONE

LEARN TO REMAIN IN HIM

Scripture Memory (new):

[28] "Come to me, all you who are weary and burdened, and I will give you rest. [29] Take my yoke upon you and learn from me, for I am gentle and humble in heart, and you will find rest for your souls. [30] For my yoke is easy and my burden is light." Matthew 11:28–30

Scripture Memory (review): Matthew 4:19

Read: John 15:1–10

MY UPBRINGING PRODUCED IN ME a sense of rugged individualism and independence. I (Bryan) have always enjoyed the sense of independence. Nothing was more enjoyable to me than a beautiful summer day with the wind and sun on my face as I hopped on my Harley-Davidson motorcycle. Talk about the freedom of the open road! But we all know that even when we feel that sense of freedom—like we can do anything in the world on our own—nothing could be further from the truth. Often in my ministry I would feel like I could do anything, even God's work, on my own. That sounds a whole lot like pride! But I have come to realize that I really can't do everything on my own. In fact, since the accident, I literally need to rely on other people to do the things I used to take for granted. And it's not easy to have to acknowledge that! But in my weakness, Christ is made strong. I know that I can't do it on my own. Both personally and pastorally, I have realized that it takes a church community to help accomplish the mission. It takes family to help provide encouragement, support, and prayer. But most of all, it takes faith in God that he will provide everything I need at just the right time and in just the right way.

John 15 describes how essential it is that we remain in Christ, staying connected to him and dependent on him as our source for life. God has a purpose for each one of our lives. His purpose is that we would fulfill his purpose (bear fruit) in his world. We are not on this planet for ourselves or to find *our* purpose. We are here for him and to fulfill *his* purpose. Jesus uses an analogy of a vine and the fruit it produces to make this point.

Who does Jesus say is the vine?

What is the role of the Father?

What is the role of the follower of Christ?

The word "remain" appears eleven times in John 15:1–10, always in reference to staying close to and connected to Jesus. I'll remind us again that following Jesus is always about staying close to Jesus, remaining in him.

What promise does Jesus give us in the first part of John 15:4?

If you remain in him, he promises to remain in you. Do you want to remain in Christ? There's a great passage in James 4:8 that says something similar: "Come near to God and he will come near to you." When you reach out to God, he will reach out to you.

One of the ways you can reach out to God and grow closer to him is through worship. To "worship" God simply means you choose to put your life in service for him. You declare to God that he is your final authority and that you want to honor him with your life. Some people find it helpful to sing to God in worship. We express our love, thankfulness, and commitment to God at our services. I encourage you to begin to do this right away. There is something power-ful that happens when you reach out to God. It is important to know that you can also do this at home. You may want to check out the list of suggested songs for each of the attributes on the website **learningtofollow.net**. These songs will sup-port you on your journey. If you need help with this, talk with your spiritual coach about it. He or she should be able to help you.

Based on John 15:1–4, why can't a follower of Jesus be a "rugged individualist?"..

We are going to explore some of the ways we can learn to remain in him in the following days, but right now you may realize, as I do, that you need to repent for trying to live life on your own without God. Why not take a few minutes right now to just enjoy your connection to Christ.

Prayer:

Dear Jesus, thank you for the invitation to follow you. It is amazing to me that you want me to remain close to you forever. I am humbled that you, the Creator of the universe, would love me and desire to be close to me and me to you. I declare that you are the final author-ity in my life and that I want to honor you with my life. Forgive me for trying to do life on my own. I turn away from trying to do life my own way and I turn to you. I accept your invitation to remain in you and your promise to remain in me. I realize that I cannot bear the kind of fruit that you have planned for my life on my own. I am here for you. Amen.

Thought for the Day:

Write out the following words "I am in you" on an index card. Look at the card throughout the day and allow your awareness of God's presence in you to affect how you do your work and life.

ATTRIBUTE ONE · STEP TWO
LEARN TO RECOGNIZE FRUIT

Scripture Memory:

²⁸ "Come to ——, all you who are —— and burdened, and I will give you ——. ²⁹ Take my —— upon you and learn from——, for I am gentle and ———— in heart, and you will find rest for your——. ³⁰ For my —— is easy and my burden is——." ————11:28–30

²⁸ "Come to me, all you who are weary and burdened, and I will give you rest. ²⁹ Take my yoke upon you and learn from me, for I am gentle and humble in heart, and you will find rest for your souls. ³⁰ For my yoke is easy and my burden is light." Matthew 11:28–30

Read: John 15:5–6; Galatians 5:22–23

I (BRYAN) LOVE FRUIT. Nothing was more refreshing on a hot summer day in North Carolina than eating a slice of cold, fresh watermelon right off the vine from my grandmother's garden. While stuffing myself full, I saved every little seed for the artillery assault that I would launch later on my sister. As I spit the sticky projectiles toward my intended target, my sister would laugh and then very quickly fire back from her personal stockpile. Talk about good fruit!

Who does Jesus say is the vine?......................

What are we?.....................................

Why do you think Jesus wants us to stay connected with the Father?

Jesus says in John 15:5, "If you remain in me and I in you, you will bear much fruit." In other words, if you stay close to God, you will bear much fruit that looks like God. Furthermore, you cannot bear godly fruit on your own. I will put it another way. If you go to an apple tree, what do you expect? If you go to a grape vine, what do you expect? The same applies to God. If you stay connected to God, what can you expect? God has summarized what his fruit is like in Galatians 5:22–23.

The fruit of the Spirit is:

* **Love**—loving people without expecting anything back, no strings attached

* **Joy**—delight, being in a good mood because God is exceptionally good or satisfying

* **Peace**—health and wholeness in relationships and personal well being

* **Patience**—prolonged restraint of anger and agitation

* **Kindness**—friendly, regardless of how people treat you

* **Goodness**—being generous and kind to people

* **Faithfulness**—confident trust in God that results in consistent actions

* **Gentleness**—humility, considerateness, meekness, preferring others

* **Self-control**—disciplined, control over actions and appetites

We need all of them, don't we?

Which of these do you need the most right now?............

What would change if God would give you that fruit?

Make whatever you mentioned above a matter of prayer. Ask God to give you his fruit in your life. When you remain in Christ, you and others will begin to see God's fruit in your life. Isn't he awesome? Like any fruit, it takes time to grow. Don't become impatient with yourself when it doesn't happen overnight. Just stay close to Jesus, delighting in him and in his Word. Trust him. When you notice some fruit, thank him for it. Enjoy the changes he is bringing about in your life.

The latter part of John 15:5 reminds us that becoming like Christ is not something we do on our own or by our own efforts. Notice that it says clearly, "Apart from me you can do nothing." Wow! So much for trying to produce godly fruit on your own! Can't do it! Don't even try it without the Lord.

Prayer:
Heavenly Father, thank you for the assurance that you are my source and that you will produce fruit in my life as I remain in you. I look forward to it. I pray that nothing in my life will inhibit your fruit from growing in me. I don't want to grow fruit so that people will look at me. I want to grow it so that people will look to you and so that you will receive the glory. Change me into your likeness, I pray. Amen.

ATTRIBUTE ONE · STEP THREE
LEARN TO BE WITH HIM AS YOU READ SCRIPTURE

Scripture Memory:

²⁸ "Come to ____ , all ____ who are ____ ____ ____ , and I will ____ ____ ____ . ²⁹ Take my ____ ____ ____ and learn ____ ____ , for I am ____ ____ ____ ____ ____ ____ , and you will ____ ____ ____ ____ ____ . ³⁰ For my ____ ____ and my ____ ____ ____ ." ____ ____ :28–30

²⁸ *"Come to me, all you who are weary and burdened, and I will give you rest.* ²⁹ *Take my yoke upon you and learn from me, for I am gentle and humble in heart, and you will find rest for your souls.* ³⁰ *For my yoke is easy and my burden is light." Matthew 11:28–30*

Read: John 15:7; John 1:1–18; Psalm 1

NOTICE JOHN 15:7, "IF YOU REMAIN IN ME and my words remain in you...." Part of remaining in him is that his words need to remain in us. Earlier in this Gospel, in John 1:1–4, the writer describes Jesus this way:

> In the beginning was the Word, and the Word was with God, and the Word was God. He was with God in the beginning. Through him all things were made; without him nothing was made that has been made. In him was life, and that life was the light of all mankind.

Then, John 1:14a states, "The Word became flesh and made his dwelling among us." The point is this: Jesus is the exact representation of what God is like. When you want to know what God is like, look at Jesus.

In order to really look at Jesus, you are going to have to read and review often the four books of the Bible that tell you specifically about Jesus (Matthew, Mark, Luke, and John). In these books, you learn how he thinks and acts in various situations.

The rest of the New Testament (Acts through Revelation) tells you how Jesus continued and continues to lead and direct his followers (the church) since his death and resurrection. But it doesn't stop there. Jesus also said that the rest of the Bible points to him as well: "Everything must be fulfilled that is written about me in the Law of Moses, the Prophets and the Psalms" (Luke 24:44). As a follower of Jesus, you will want to eventually read and study the entire Bible so you can allow his words to remain in you.

The idea of reading and studying the whole Bible may seem like a huge task right now. Don't let it overwhelm you. Just read a little bit each day and apply it to your life. As you begin to develop your quiet time with God, I recommend you do the following:

- Set a regular time and a place. It should be a quiet and a private place. Remember Jesus' words in Matthew 6:6: "But when you pray, go into your room, close the door and pray to your Father, who is unseen. Then your Father, who sees what is done in secret, will reward you." I like the morning because it helps me start the day off right. Some prefer the evening. The important thing is that you make regular time for God. What time and place works best for you?

- Decide on a Bible reading plan.
  - Read straight through an entire book of the Bible, one at a time, at your own pace. I encourage you to start with the Gospel of Matthew since that is our primary textbook.

→ Don't read so much that you cannot reflect on its meaning. Many people start with a chapter a day.[1]

→ Don't jump around as you read, reading a few verses here and there in that book or another book. You will be better able to understand what you are reading if you read it in context.

• Pray for guidance before you start reading. Ask Jesus to guide you into truth through his Word. Remember, he is with you.

• Make notes of what you notice and what you think God may be speaking to you as you read. I have a small notebook in which I write these things. I also underline verses that stand out to me. These serve as a living testimony of my relationship with Christ. I highly recommend you do something similar.

• Prayerfully respond to what you are reading. If you notice something in your life needs to change, pray that God will help you change it. If you notice an aspect of God that is encouraging, thank God for it. If an action is needed, ask God for wisdom in how to carry out the action.

• Remember your focus is on Jesus and not the habit of having a quiet time.

Prayer:

Dear Jesus, thank you for providing a way for me to remain in you through your Word. Open my mind to your thoughts and your ways and your ideas. Teach me how to remain in your words so you can bear your fruit through me. Help me to set aside a specific time each day at _____ to meet with you and to read your Word. I rest in your guidance. Amen.

ATTRIBUTE ONE · STEP FOUR
LEARN TO BE WITH CHRIST
IN PRAYER

Scripture Memory:

²⁸ "Come ___ ___, all ___ ___ ___ ___ ___ ___, and I ___ ___ ___ ___. ²⁹ Take ___ ___ ___ ___ ___ ___ ___, for ___ ___ ___ ___ ___ ___, and you ___ ___ ___ ___ ___. ³⁰ For ___ ___ ___ ___ ___ ___ ___ ___ ___." ___ ___ ___:___ – ___

²⁸ "Come to me, all you who are weary and burdened, and I will give you rest. ²⁹ Take my yoke upon you and learn from me, for I am gentle and humble in heart, and you will find rest for your souls. ³⁰ For my yoke is easy and my burden is light." Matthew 11:28–30

Read: John 15:7; Matthew 7:7–12; James 4:2–3

IN THE PREVIOUS STEP, WE FOCUSED on the first half of John 15:7 that reminded us of the importance of remaining connected with God. In this step, we are focusing on the effect this has on our prayer life: "If you remain in me and my words remain in you, ask whatever you wish, and it will be done for you."

When you remain in Jesus and remain in his Word, you will learn to pray his kind of prayers, and God will answer them. Prayer is not like a magic genie. It is not about saying the right words and "presto," getting your wish. The Lord does not give you everything you want or everything you ask for.

What does James 4:2–3 say are the reasons why some prayers are not answered?

The invitation is to get close to Jesus so you know the things about which he cares most. When you align your heart with his desires, there is an open-endedness about what can happen in prayer. God values your creativity. He says that if you remain in him and in his Word, then you can ask him for what is in your heart. I have heard my friend Dr. Don Meyer say on many occasions, "If you please to do as God pleases, you can do as you please." I think Jesus would say, "If you will pray as I please, then you can pray as you please." There is a whole world of discovery between you and God. Stay close to him and start asking him for great things for his kingdom. He just might say, "Great idea!" and make it happen.

It is important to know that God answers your prayers. I think it was my mother who first told me that sometimes God answers "Yes." Sometimes he says "No." And sometimes he says "Not yet." But God is always good and it should never be said of you that you don't have because you simply did not ask.

In Matthew 7:7–11, Jesus says something similar:

> Ask and it will be given to you; seek and you will find; knock and the door will be opened to you. For everyone who asks receives; the one who seeks finds; and to the one who knocks, the door will be opened. Which of you, if your son asks for bread, will give him a stone? Or if he asks for a fish, will give him a snake? If you, then, though you are evil, know how to give good gifts to your children, how much more will your Father in heaven give good gifts to those who ask him!

In short, stay close to the Lord to learn his heart. Pray Jesus' kind of prayers and you can count on your good heavenly Father to answer them.

I have talked with some people who think they should pray only when they absolutely have to, as if you only get so many answered prayers in your life so you had better save them for when you really need them. That is not how God is! He tells us to ask. That's not my idea. Those are his words. Ask! Just ask!

All this talk about asking makes me want to talk with God right now. Got anything on your mind you would like him to answer? Why not talk with him about it? I have modeled some of my prayers up to this point. It's time for you to fly solo a little bit. I'll help you with suggestions.

Prayer:
1. Talk with God like you would a good friend.
2. Thank God for what he is doing in your life right now.
3. If something about this lesson stood out to you, talk with him about it.
4. Ask God in your own words for the things that are on your mind and then tell him that you will trust him.

ATTRIBUTE ONE · STEP FIVE

LEARN HOW REMAINING IN CHRIST AFFECTS OTHERS

Scripture Memory:

28 "_____ _____ , _____ _____ ,
_____ . 29 _____ _____
_____ , _____ _____ ,
_____ . 30 _____ _____ : _____ — _____

²⁸ *"Come to me, all you who are weary and burdened, and I will give you rest.* ²⁹ *Take my yoke upon you and learn from me, for I am gentle and humble in heart, and you will find rest for your souls.* ³⁰ *For my yoke is easy and my burden is light." Matthew 11:28–30*

Read: John 15:9–12

I WISH IT WEREN'T TRUE but there are some people who claim to be followers of Christ who are simply awful to be around. They are flat-out negative. They seem to have the attitude that serving the Lord is a burden they have to bear. They have made a decision to get through it, kind of like you get through a root canal. I don't know what Bible they are reading, but that's not what Jesus had in mind for his followers, as this passage attests.

First, Jesus reminds us of how much he loves us, "As the Father has loved me, so have I loved you." We see glimpses of the Father's love for his Son, Jesus, throughout the Scriptures. At Jesus' baptism, the Father affirms his love for the Son. He says, "This is my Son, whom I love; with him I am well pleased" (Matthew 3:17). Then, when Jesus was momentarily changed on the mountain, the Father again declares his love for Jesus, "This is my Son, whom I love; with him I am well pleased. Listen to him!" (Matthew 17:5). In Jesus' prayer right before he died, several times he mentions God's amazing love for him, "I have made you known to them, and will continue to make you known in order that the love you have for me may be in them and that I myself may be in them" (John 17:26). Jesus said simply that the love he received from the Father, he has given to us. He just calls us to remain in that love. Then, Jesus tells us how to remain in his love.

How do we remain in his love according to verse 10?

According to verse 12, what is his command?

This is the part that my friends who are not enjoying Jesus don't get. It's not a huge burden to give away something so wonderful as the love of Jesus.

Did someone ever give you a special gift? Perhaps it was tickets to a special athletic event or a great vacation that you couldn't afford. Perhaps someone gave his time when you needed it the most. I (Daniel) can think of lots of these, but one stands out to me right now. I was going through a difficult struggle just after we moved to Texas when I was in high school. I had a sister who was twelve years older than I who lived in Wisconsin at that time with her husband. Because she knew me and wanted me to know I was loved, she used to send me packages with special greeting cards and articles about Christian athletes and other kinds of things about which I was interested. At the time, I was too "cool" to communicate how much those expressions of love meant to me, but I looked for them in the mail. I read every article she sent. It was a lifeline to a fifteen-year-old who needed to know he was loved. Then, to top it off, she would call me, or my parents would let me call her sometimes, and she would take the time with me to talk about what was on my mind. It really helped me get through a tough time. Here's my point: after I got through that time, I thought about how caring my sister was, and it made me want to be like that for others. I want to do for others what I experienced. It's not a big burden, because I know what being cared for feels like.

That's all Jesus is saying in this passage. Just give away the love you are experiencing from him. It's not a burden. In fact, it is just the opposite. It's fun. It brings you joy. Jesus says in verse 11, "I have told you this so that my joy may be in you and that your joy may be complete." His command is just that we would love others like he has loved us. Remaining in Christ's love will cause you to want to give his love away to others. The more you receive from him, the more you are going to want to give away.

Sometimes my heart goes out to "Christians" who are not having fun following Jesus. I wonder if they have ever stayed in Christ's presence long enough to experience his extravagant love. Let that never be said of you. You now know the secret of the joyful Christian life. Stay close to Jesus and give away what he gives to you. He will change the world around you if you will do that.

Prayer:

Draw me close to you, Jesus. Thank you for your amazing love and friendship. Help me to give away to others what you have given to me so the world will know you are real and that you love them.

ATTRIBUTE ONE
DECISIONS

ATTRIBUTE TWO

• • •

LEARN TO LISTEN

ATTRIBUTE TWO
INTRODUCTION
LEARN TO LISTEN

IT IS SIGNIFICANT THAT THE FIRST THING Jesus did after calling his disciples to follow him was to invite them to listen and watch as he taught in the synagogues and healed people (Matthew 4:23–25). I probably would have expected him to take some time to build a relationship and to teach them privately. Not Jesus. He took them right into the middle of real ministry where they could hear his words and see them put into practice right away.

As you are learning to listen to Jesus, it is important to know he will speak to you in four ways: through his written Word (the Bible); through prayer; in circumstances; and through his people, the church.

Furthermore, hearing Jesus' words is not enough. You need to **do** what he says. Matthew 7:24–25 records Jesus words:

> Therefore everyone who **hears** these words of mine and **puts them into practice** is like a wise man who built his house on the rock. The rain came down, the streams rose, and the winds blew and beat against that house; yet it did not fall, because it had its foundation on the rock. [Emphasis mine.]

As a follower of Jesus, you will want to be in settings where you can hear the teachings of Jesus and see him change lives. Acts 2:46 describes the earliest followers of Jesus meeting regularly in large gatherings (the temple courts) and in small groups (homes). We need both. That's why we have both large groups (worship services) and the small groups. At our Sunday services, we worship God, hear his Word taught, and serve others. It's also a great place to bring a friend who wants to see what following Christ is all about. In our small groups, we ask questions, encourage one another, and learn how to hear and apply God's Word to our daily lives. We also have Jesus' assurance that he is with us in a special way, "For where two or three gather in my name, there am I with them" (Matthew 18:20). In both size groups, however, it is really important to focus on learning to hear the words of Jesus so you can put them into practice.

Besides a large service and a small group, it is also important to learn to hear Jesus by reading the Bible. One of the challenges I (Daniel) experienced in learning to follow Jesus was that I thought I already knew the Bible. I was raised in a Christian home and we went to church often. We also usually read at least a small portion of the Bible together as a family at the breakfast table, and we prayed before we left in the morning. I am grateful for my Christian heritage. Although I invited Christ into my life as a child many times just to make sure I would go to heaven, I became a follower of Jesus in the latter part of high school. I knew a lot about God. God had been with me all my life, but I did not know him very well personally.

As a child, one of my (Bryan's) favorite go-to Bible stories was David and Goliath. Growing up I can remember my mom reading that story from the "blue Bible books" and from the Bible itself on occasion, but I was raised in a home where we went to church often and read the Bible seldom. One of the challenges I experienced in learning to follow Jesus was realizing I didn't really understand the Bible. When I received Christ during my junior year in high school, I began to read the Bible on a daily basis. Because of a lack of spiritual coaching my Bible studies began with the book of Zechariah where I read of visions and flying scrolls (probably not the best place for a new Christian to start). Even though it was fun to read these stories, I still felt like I was missing a lot of the message. The few people who were trying to help me in my faith told me that in order to grow I needed to attend church, pray often, and read the Bible. That was true to a degree, but everyone needs help from others in order to develop as a Christ follower in those areas. As we commit our lives to God the most exciting discovery of this journey of faith is that Christ says he will never leave us or forsake us.

In this lesson we are going to focus on learning to carefully hear the words of Jesus in the Scriptures so you can put them into practice. Besides attending a corporate worship service and a small group, I am encouraging you to set aside at least fifteen minutes each day for "hearing" time. As you learn to hear the Word of God, you need to develop the habit of "doing" it right way. There should not be a lengthy time between "hearing" and "doing." Jesus expects you to act on what you know. You don't need to learn a lot each day, just enough so you can apply it to your life that day.

We'll talk more about this throughout the lesson, but I would like to give you some advice:

+ Choose a Bible reading plan that works for you. I suggest reading the passages in this guide as your reading for now. You may want to read the entire book of Matthew when you are done. After that you might want to work your way through the New Testament. The important thing is that you make Bible reading a normal part of your day.

+ Pray before you start reading. Ask God to point out things to you. Don't rush through your Bible reading. Read with an open heart.

+ When something stands out to you, underline it in your Bible. It is easy to go back and review if it is marked in some way.

→ Write down what stood out to you. I use a simple loose-leaf notebook to record my thoughts. Even though I have just underlined it in my Bible, I often write out the passage longhand in my notebook. It slows me down, and I think about it as I am writing. Then, I prayerfully write about why I think that passage applies to me right now. God often gives me a fresh perspective on a specific situation I am facing that day.

→ Pray. Ask God how he wants you to act on what stood out to you that day. Some days you will have something significant to apply. At other times, you will have something to think about. The important thing is that you read and apply it right away.

You may want to reflect with your coach about how your devotional time is going. Don't give up on the process if you are struggling with consistency. Developing a new habit takes time and effort. Most people say it takes twenty-one days to make a new habit. Stay with it. Just do it. I believe you will find God's Word to have a powerful influence on your life if you will develop the habit of learning to listen.

When will you do your Bible reading and "listening" time?...

Are you involved in a small group? If so, how is it going?

Prayer:

Lord, help me to learn to listen to your words so I can apply them to the life you have given me. I want to build a foundation that will last when the storms of life come. I want you to be the cornerstone of my life from this day onward. Help me to faithfully apply your Word to my life. Help me to be a doer of your Word and not just a hearer. I ask this in Jesus' name, amen.

ATTRIBUTE TWO · STEP ONE

LEARN TO BE HAPPY

Scripture Memory (new):

24 "Therefore everyone who hears these words of mine and puts them into practice is like a wise man who built his house on the rock. 25 The rain came down, the streams rose, and the winds blew and beat against that house; yet it did not fall, because it had its foundation on the rock." Matthew 7:24–25

Scripture Memory (review): Matthew 4:19
Matthew 11:28–30

Read: Matthew 5:1–12

WHAT WORDS ARE REPEATED in Matthew 5:1–12?

Each of the nine statements in this section begins with Jesus saying, "Blessed." Some translators actually translate the word *blessed* as "happy." This is not a bad translation, but the English word *happy* is too shallow for what the word means. I'll do my best to explain what *blessed* means below.

> In secular Greece the island of Cyprus was called the blest island. The idea was that those who lived in Cyprus never had to leave its shores in order to have all they needed to be content…the island was self-contained. No one had to search for the needs and wants of life.[1]

That's partly what *blessed* means—when you have it, you

are fortunate and satisfied and you don't have to look elsewhere for it.

The Old Testament meaning of *blessed* meant you were approved by God. In other words, you can't be a blessed person and not be approved by God. "When we are blessed by God, our happiness does not come from circumstances, or by accident, or through a diligent search. It comes because we stand approved before the Creator of the universe."[2]

According to these verses, who is blessed?

Does anything surprise you about those who are blessed?

In these verses, Jesus teaches us the truth, not as our world teaches, but something we would never discover on our own. He teaches that blessing is not linked to how much you have in this world. Blessed people are those who realize they have nothing to bring to God, the poor in spirit. If you discover that truth, regardless of your economic reality, you literally will receive it all—the kingdom of heaven, the mother lode of all gifts. Blessing is for everyone who knows the truth about what he or she has before God. We have nothing to offer him except our lives and he has everything to offer us. These verses illustrate how important it is to come to Christ to learn from him what life, blessing, and everything else in life is all about.

What kinds of things do you tend to rely on to find your sense of worth and value?

How might your life be different if you found all of your significance and value in God?

With these verses Jesus offers blessing and hope for every

person on the planet. For those who are mourning, he promises comfort. For those who prefer others ahead of themselves (the meek), he promises a huge inheritance. For those who are hungry and thirsty to do right things (righteousness), he promises they will be satisfied. For those who are merciful, he promises mercy. For those who are pure in heart, he promises an audience with God. For those who seek peace, he promises to call them his family. For those who are persecuted in this life, he promises that God's kingdom belongs to them. They get it all. For those who are insulted and spoken against, Jesus says they can rejoice because they are in great company; that's what happened to the prophets and eventually to Jesus as well. You simply cannot lose when you find everything in God.

Take a few moments to think about how you have nothing except your life to offer God. You may even want to close your eyes and turn your open palms upward as a symbol of your poverty of spirit. Now talk with God about that.

Prayer:
Heavenly Father, I realize I have nothing to offer you except my life. Although it is broken and messed up, it is all I have. If you can do something with it, please take it. I realize I am poor in spirit but you say that I am blessed because of that. That's very encouraging to me. It gives me hope. The ground is level before you. I come to you the same as every other person under your leadership comes: empty-handed. You give me everything. I receive your kingdom in my life. You are so good. Have your way in my life.

ATTRIBUTE TWO · STEP TWO
LEARN TO GO TO THE SOURCE

Scripture Memory:

²⁴ "Therefore _____ who hears these_____ of mine and
puts them into_____ is like a_____ man who built his
_____ on the rock. ²⁵ The_____ came down, the streams
_____, and the winds blew and_____against that house; yet
it did not_____, because it had its _____ on the rock."
_____ 7:24–25

*²⁴ "Therefore everyone who hears these words of mine and puts
them into practice is like a wise man who built his house on the
rock. ²⁵ The rain came down, the streams rose, and the winds
blew and beat against that house; yet it did not fall, because it
had its foundation on the rock." Matthew 7:24–25*

Read: 2 Timothy 3:16–17

READING THE SCRIPTURE WILL BE AN IMPORTANT PART
of your growth as a follower of Christ. 2 Timothy 3:16–
17 describes what makes Scripture so important and the
significant role it will have in your life as a follower.
What claim does 2 Timothy 3:16 make?

"God-breathed" means "inspired by God." It means
that God communicated his message through the thoughts
and vocabulary of the human writers. It doesn't mean he

"dictated" it, but it does mean that God directed the writer even in the selection of his words so that God's intent and purpose come through. It's amazing to realize that God has given us in writing his thoughts in human language. Pretty cool.

In what four ways does this passage say that Scripture can help you? Write them below.

....

....

If you wrote teaching, rebuking, correcting and training in righteousness, you are correct. Scripture will help you learn information about God and how to follow Christ (teaching). It will help you discover things you are doing that you need to do differently (rebuking). It will help you restore and reestablish your foundation so you can be who you were designed to be (correcting). And, it will help train and discipline you to honor God with your life and actions (training in righteousness). Isn't it great that you can know where to find the answers to those life questions?

What is your plan to incorporate Bible reading into your life? Share this with your spiritual coach when you get together. ....

....

Do you have specific questions about God for which you could use an answer? Your spiritual coach may or may not know the answers, but one of the leaders of the church will help steer you in the right direction. What are your questions? ....

....

Do you have questions about what it means to be a follower of Jesus? What are they? ....

....

....

Are there things you are doing in your life that you are aware need God's help to change now that you are a follower of Jesus? ....

....

....

Do you feel you need restoration in a certain area of your life so you can build a solid foundation with God? ....

....

God is in the process of changing your life and mine. He loves you with an everlasting love. There is nothing you can do to make God love you more or make him love you less. But God loves you too much to leave you where you are. He wants you to become all that he has designed you to become. For that to happen, he needs to change you. There is your work and there is his work. Your work is to ask God and to submit yourself to him. It is God's will to change you into his likeness. That will happen as you systematically put yourself in a situation to hear God's Word and to put it into practice. Call to mind again Jesus' words in Matthew 7:24–25:

> Therefore everyone who hears these words of mine and puts them into practice is like a wise man who built his house on the rock. The rain came down, the streams rose, and the winds blew and beat against that house; yet it did not fall, because it had its foundation on the rock.

What decision(s) are you making today? ....

....

Prayer:

Heavenly Father, thank you for your Word that guides me into truth. Help me to make the Scriptures part of my everyday life. With your help, I am going to attempt to read the Bible each day. I need to know your thoughts so I can know how to please you and live the life you have designed me to live. I ask for your help with this. I want to please you. Amen.

ATTRIBUTE TWO · STEP THREE
LEARN TO SEE JESUS IN SCRIPTURE

Scripture Memory:

²⁴ "Therefore _____ who _____ these _____ of mine and
_____ them into _____ is like a _____ man who_____ his
_____ on the _____. ²⁵ The _____ _____ _____, the streams
_____, and the_____ and _____against that house; yet
it____ ___ _____, because it had its _____ on the _____."
_____ ___ :24–25

---

²⁴ *"Therefore everyone who hears these words of mine and puts
them into practice is like a wise man who built his house on the
rock. ²⁵ The rain came down, the streams rose, and the winds
blew and beat against that house; yet it did not fall, because it
had its foundation on the rock." Matthew 7:24–25*

Read: Luke 24:13–49

WHAT STANDS OUT TO YOU about these accounts?...........

....

After Jesus' resurrection from the dead he appeared to
his disciples. Jesus said something very interesting in Luke
24:44, "Everything must be fulfilled that is written about me
in the Law of Moses, the Prophets and the Psalms." Verse 45
says, "Then he opened their minds so they could understand
the Scriptures." At least two things are important about this.
First, Jesus pointed his followers to read the Scriptures to

understand who he was. Second, Jesus helped them understand by opening their minds. Both are true for you and other followers of Jesus.

It might be helpful to learn some basic things about the Bible. Open your Bible to the front cover and turn each page until you find what looks like a table of contents. You will notice that the Bible is made up of two parts: the Old Testament and the New Testament. The Old Testament was written down and took place before the life of Jesus. The New Testament was written by his followers after Jesus' resurrection.

The Old Testament is made up of five main parts: the Pentateuch which is the first five books of the Bible (Genesis through Deuteronomy), the Historical Books (Joshua through Esther), Psalms and Wisdom Literature (Job through Song of Songs), the Major Prophets (Isaiah, Jeremiah, and Ezekiel) and the Minor Prophets (Lamentations and Daniel through Malachi).

The New Testament is made up five main parts as well: Gospels (Matthew through John), Acts, Pauline Epistles (Romans through Philemon), General Epistles (Hebrews through Jude), and Revelation.

Jesus said in essence, "All Scripture points to me." This is helpful for us because anytime you are reading a passage of Scripture, even if it is perhaps confusing, you can ask, "How does this point to Jesus?" And you will be asking the right question.

The writer of Hebrews said this about Jesus: "The Son is the radiance of God's glory and the exact representation of his being, sustaining all things by his powerful word" (Hebrews 1:3).

Jesus came to change our lives. When we read Scripture under his direction, he lovingly and strongly guides us into a new way of life.

Prayer

As we conclude today, rather than praying my prayer, I want to pray over you the prayer the Apostle Paul prayed for the new followers of Jesus in Colossians 1:9–18:

> [9] For this reason, since the day we heard about you, we have not stopped praying for you. We continually ask God to fill you with the knowledge of his will through all the wisdom and understanding that the Spirit gives, [10] so that you may live a life worthy of the Lord and please him in every way: bearing fruit in every good work, growing in the knowledge of God, [11] being strengthened with all power according to his glorious might so that you may have great endurance and patience, [12] and giving joyful thanks to the Father, who has qualified you to share in the inheritance of his holy people in the kingdom of light. [13] For he has rescued us from the dominion of darkness and brought us into the kingdom of the Son he loves, [14] in whom we have redemption, the forgiveness of sins. [15] The Son is the image of the invisible God, the firstborn over all creation. [16] For in him all things were created: things in heaven and on earth, visible and invisible, whether thrones or powers or rulers or authorities; all things have been created through him and for him. [17] He is before all things, and in him all things hold together. [18] And he is the head of the body, the church; he is the beginning and the firstborn from among the dead, so that in everything he might have the supremacy.

I look forward to hearing the stories of how God changes your life through the power of his Word.

ATTRIBUTE TWO · STEP FOUR
LEARN TO OVERCOME TEMPTATION

Scripture Memory:

[24] "Therefore ___ ___ ___ these ___ of ___ and ___ ___ into ___ is like a ___ ___ who ___ his ___ on the ___. [25] The ___ ___ ___, the ___ ___, and the ___ and ___ against that ___; yet it ___ ___, because ___ ___ ___ ___ on the ___."
Matthew 7:__ – __

[24] *"Therefore everyone who hears these words of mine and puts them into practice is like a wise man who built his house on the rock. [25] The rain came down, the streams rose, and the winds blew and beat against that house; yet it did not fall, because it had its foundation on the rock." Matthew 7:24–25*

Read: Matthew 4:1–11

FIND IT VERY ENCOURAGING that Jesus doesn't just talk about what people ought to do. He shows us how to live and then tells us to do the same. In Matthew 4, Jesus was led by the Spirit into the desert to be tempted by the devil. Do you want to know how to handle temptation? Do you want to know how to succeed every time when you are tempted? Take note of Jesus.

Jesus was tempted in three ways. According to Matthew 4:2–3, about what was the first temptation? ....

Can you think of some ways you are tempted by normal human appetites?

How did Jesus overcome this temptation?

If your Bible has references, you will see a note to let you know Jesus quoted Deuteronomy 8:3. When Jesus was tempted to use divine power to meet his own physical needs, he remembered the biblical principle that God is responsible for sustaining us by his Word. We exist because God said it. We are here by God and for God and not the other way around. We must submit even our human appetites to God. He will meet them in his way and at his time. It is all a gift from him. Jesus knew this principle because he knew the Word of God. It was in his heart and mind so he did not sin when tempted to do his own thing.

According to Matthew 4:5–6, what did the devil tempt Jesus to do?

By what means did the devil try to convince Jesus he should do this?

Isn't it amazing that the devil even used Scripture on Jesus? The devil knows how powerful Scripture is, but he did something that you should see. He quoted Scripture to make it say what he wanted it to say rather than what God intended it to mean. He cleverly quoted a portion of Psalm 91 out of context, "For he will command his angels concerning you to guard you...they will lift you up in their hands, so that you will not strike your foot against a stone" (vv. 11–12). In context, however, Psalm 91:9 states, "If you make the Most High your dwelling...then no harm will befall you." God's protection comes when we live for him, not when we do foolish things. Be careful to read Scripture for what it says, not what you want it to say.

Notice again that Jesus quoted Scripture to respond to the devil's temptation. See if you can find in the marginal reference in your Bible which passage Jesus quoted.[1] Jesus was tempted to prove he was the Son of God by doing a spectacular sign. God never shows off. Asking God to do that is way out of line. Jesus knew that, because he knew the Word of God, and he could quote it when tempted. You can do the same as you learn God's Word.

What was the main topic of the devil's third temptation for Jesus according to Matthew 4:8–9? ....

Jesus knew he had to suffer and die a cruel death in order to save the whole world. All he had to do was bow down one time to the devil, and he could have the glory without the cross. There are no shortcuts to the will of God. Jesus knew that because he knew the Word of God. We were created to worship only God. I wanted to use these examples because we find in them our example for how to handle temptation. We need to know the truth of God's Word in context so we can apply it to our lives.

There are no shortcuts to following Jesus and to being able to handle temptations when they come. You need to know the truth of God's Word in context. You need daily infusions of God's Word to be able to live the life God has for you. How is your Bible reading going? ....

> **Prayer:**
> Heavenly Father, thank you for your Word that teaches me how to live and to overcome temptation. I would not be able to know you personally if it were not for Jesus Christ. His example and your Word in context shows what you are like and what you think. Thank you for sending both to me to show me the way back to you. Help me to prioritize reading and applying your Word to my life daily. Amen.

ATTRIBUTE TWO · STEP FIVE
LEARN TO BE PRODUCTIVE

Scripture Memory:

24 " ___ ___ ___ ___ ___ ___ ___

___ ___ ___ ___ ___ ___ ___

___ ___ ___ ___ . 25 ___ ___ ___ , ___

___ , ___ ___ ___ ___ ___ ___ ; ___

___ ___ ___ , ___ ___ ___ ___ . "

___ ___ : ___ – ___

24 "Therefore everyone who hears these words of mine and puts them into practice is like a wise man who built his house on the rock. 25 The rain came down, the streams rose, and the winds blew and beat against that house; yet it did not fall, because it had its foundation on the rock." Matthew 7:24–25

Read: Luke 8:5–15

I (DANIEL) USED TO HAVE A BIG VEGETABLE GARDEN. I loved to see plants grow, but I also loved to eat what I grew. There is nothing like a vine-ripened tomato, fresh green beans, and homemade salsa from all fresh ingredients. My mouth is watering just thinking about it.

There are several keys to a productive garden. You need the right seeds or starter plants, the right amount of water and sun, protection from pests, and good soil. Many people know about the first three but fail to make sure the soil is prepared properly. It is amazing how much more can be produced if you prepare the soil properly before you plant.

Jesus taught in Luke 8 how the soil of our hearts makes all the difference in our productivity as his followers. What four types of soil did Jesus describe?

He taught about four kinds of heart soils: hard ground, rocky soil, thorny soil, and good soil. Each soil receives the same seed, has the same amount of water and sunlight, and the same exposure to pests, but some never produce at all. Some start to produce but don't make it, some look pretty good but never produce, and others produce greatly. The only difference is the soil.

What does Jesus say is the seed? (Luke 8:11)

What keeps the soil on the path from producing? (Luke 8:12)

What keeps the rocky soil from producing? (Luke 8:13)

What keeps the thorny soil from producing? (Luke 8:14)

What are the characteristics of the person's heart soil that produces greatly? (Luke 8:15)

Does the parable of the soil help you identify anything that could keep you from being productive in your walk with Jesus? If so, what is it and what would you like to do about it?

God's word will change your life if you are willing to tend the soil of your heart. One of the biggest challenges that many Americans face is the thorn of materialism. Some sacrifice many things (time, energy, sleep, even relationships) so they can own more material goods or have pleasurable experiences. Jesus says our productivity in the kingdom of God can be choked out by worries, riches, and pleasures. God's plan for your life is that you would be a productive follower of Jesus, that your life would count big time for his kingdom. This would be a great time to tell the Lord that you want to surrender your desires and your resources to him. The One who made you knows how to make your life productive. Wouldn't it be a shame to live your whole life and never fulfill the reason why you are here? Wouldn't it be sad to live your life for things that won't matter five seconds after you die? I don't want to do that. I want to hear my Lord say to me one day, "Well done, good and faithful servant." I'm sure you do as well.

Why don't you take a few minutes right now to write out some things you need to adjust. When you have done that, talk to God about each item. Ask him to show you how to cultivate your heart's soil so you produce a hundredfold for him.

Talk to your spiritual coach about what you feel God is directing you to change. Ask him how following Jesus has made a difference in his priorities in life. He may have some valuable insights into how to align your life to God's values.

ATTRIBUTE TWO
DECISIONS

ATTRIBUTE THREE

• • •

LEARN TO HEAL

ATTRIBUTE THREE
INTRODUCTION
LEARN TO HEAL

"**B**RYAN, WHAT IS HAPPENING IN YOUR BODY isn't just amazing, it's miraculous." Those were the words that my doctor spoke to me after I woke up from a two-week medically induced coma. After nineteen surgeries and receiving thirty-six units of blood, for anyone to call what happened to me a miracle seemed almost impossible. To think that I was going to be facing life without my wife of twenty-eight years and my left leg seemed unfathomable. Have you ever experienced something that has caused you to say that moving forward seemed impossible? A diagnosis, a failed marriage, an addiction?

As we continue to learn what it means to "follow" Jesus, we are going to take a closer look at the subject of healing. Healing was and is an integral part of the ministry of Jesus Christ. Jesus wants us to be used in the healing ministry, but first we need to experience healing. We often think of healing in terms of the physical realm, which certainly is a part of God's promise, but what is to be said for emotional healing, specifically when there is a delay of physical healing?

I've already described the dramatic healing of my right eye in 2006 and the healing I experienced in my body as a result of the accident in June of 2015, but you may ask, as I did, what about the left eye? Why did God allow me to lose my leg? These are the very questions I get asked over and over by both Christians and people that are far from God.

Faith and trust are very closely connected to healing. As followers of Christ we need to have faith that God is capable of performing what seems to be impossible. The Word of God underscores the fact that God is willing and able to heal. I also need to be able to trust God in his sovereign plan for my life. I can remember lying on my bed in the hospital room after waking up almost two weeks after my accident and learning that both Lynn and my left leg were gone. I found myself once again on the corner of "Bitter Street and Better Avenue." I remember crying out to God and asking why this and why now. I have great faith that God's grace is sufficient for me when the answer I'm looking for doesn't come. I look back now and say, "with everything that I've been through, never once did I ever walk alone." I'm glad I continue every day to walk down "Better Avenue" and allow God to heal me emotionally and physically and fulfill his plan in my life. What I have learned most through my experiences, both early in my life and recently, is that if God brings you to it, he *will* bring you through it.

When I (Daniel) was in college I lifted weights to try to improve my athletic performance. One day when I went in to lift, I saw a bar with more weight than I had ever lifted on the bottom of a squat rack. For some reason and without warming up (the logic still defies me), I decided to try to get under it and try to move it. When I pushed for all I was worth, I heard a popping/ripping sound in my lower abdomen. I went to see our doctor, and sure enough, I had a hernia. Stupid, stupid, stupid! He suggested operating right away but I talked him out of it. The basketball season was only a few weeks away and an operation would keep me out of action for about two months. I had to go back to him several times throughout the season. Each time he confirmed my hernia was getting larger. I was able to limp my way through the season, but I planned on having the surgery during spring break. A week or so before spring break, we had special meetings at the college in which the speaker encouraged us to pray for healing if we needed it. I stood to be prayed for. A student placed his hand on my shoulder and asked God to heal me. I thought I felt something warm on the spot of my hernia but I didn't tell anyone. I was not sure so I said nothing and continued with the plan for the surgery. I went to the surgeon a day before the surgery. He checked me and he could not find the hernia. He was quite perturbed because he had planned on a surgery and it wasn't needed. I heard him call the general practitioner and ask him why he sent me. After that phone call, I told the surgeon that I believed I was healed. He just looked at me, but I could tell that was way outside his box. He sent me back to my general practitioner who was baffled. I felt obligated to tell him that I thought I was healed. He said something like, "Prayer is a good thing." I was able to return immediately to full athletic activities, including weight lifting, without a problem. God had healed me.

I told you that story for a couple of reasons. First, you need to know that a rational, twenty-first century human being believes he experienced a miracle. Hernias don't heal themselves. The doctor had diagnosed and confirmed I had a hernia multiple times that year. Second, healings don't always happen immediately. I prayed for my hernia to be healed many times before God did it. I do not understand why God heals some immediately, some later, and some never at all. For instance, God did not heal my knee when I tore the anterior cruciate ligament, among other things. But the Bible teaches us that God heals and he invites us to ask.

In these sessions, as you read a variety of miracle stories, it is our hope that you will not only be open to God's divine intervention but that your faith would grow. If there is a God and if he is as the Bible describes, then God can suspend natural laws at any time to do the supernatural. Jesus said,

Ask and it will be given to you; seek and you will find; knock and the door will be opened to you. For everyone who asks receives; the one who seeks finds; and to the one who knocks, the door will be opened. (Matthew 7:7–8)

Ask.

Prayer:

Heavenly Father, you spoke and the world came into existence out of nothing. You said, "Let there be light," and there was light. That is so far beyond anything I can understand. Show me what's real about healing, and hereafter in my life, I want everything you have for me. Amen.

ATTRIBUTE THREE · STEP ONE
THE IMPORTANCE OF TOUCH

Scripture Memory (new):

[7] "Ask and it will be given to you; seek and you will find; knock and the door will be opened to you. [8] For everyone who asks receives; the one who seeks finds; and to the one who knocks, the door will be opened." Matthew 7:7–8

Scripture Memory (review): Matthew 4:19
Matthew 11:28–30   Matthew 7:24–25

Read: Matthew 4:18–22

IT IS SIGNIFICANT THAT THE FIRST THING JESUS DID after calling his disciples to follow him was to invite them to hear him teach about God's kingdom and to watch him heal people. From the beginning of their walk with Jesus, they would know that when Jesus is around, anything is possible. Matthew 4:23–24 reads this way:

> Jesus went throughout Galilee, teaching in their synagogues, preaching the good news of the kingdom, and healing every disease and sickness among the people. News about him spread all over Syria, and people brought to him all who were ill with various diseases, those suffering severe pain, the demon-possessed, those having seizures, and the paralyzed, and he healed them.

How do you think it might have affected the early

disciples to see Jesus healing people? ....

According to a survey conducted by Time Magazine, 69 percent of Americans believe in miracles.[1] Do you believe in miracles? Why or why not? ....

There are many miracles recorded in the Bible, but one moves me emotionally more than the rest. Read Matthew 8:1–4. We see Jesus going to the fringe of society; he did this every day. If we are following him, we will too.

Several things move me about this story. First, the man was desperate. There was no known cure for leprosy. They no doubt thought about it much like we think of cancer or HIV. Lepers were required to live outside the community. They also had to communicate they were diseased by how they dressed, and they had to keep to themselves (Leviticus 13:45–46; Numbers 5:1–4). Furthermore, sometimes leprosy was a direct punishment from God (Numbers 12:10; 2 Kings 5:27). The normal person wanted nothing to do with a leper for obvious reasons. Somehow the man in Matthew 8 heard about Jesus. He came and knelt before Jesus and said, "… if you are willing, you can make me clean." The depth of need, the humility, the hope demonstrated, all move me. But I think it is the next thing that moves me the most. "Jesus reached out his hand and touched the man." What? Jesus touched the man with the skin disease? Yes, Jesus touched someone who hadn't been touched in who knows how long, perhaps in years. Jesus' heart broke for one who was alone, an outcast, outside of community; one whose body was riddled with disease. He touched him. That's what God is like. His heart is moved by our brokenness. He knows what we are going through, the visible and the invisible, and he cares. The man was not just another notch in Jesus' healing belt. The man with leprosy was a person with a broken life who needed to be touched by his Creator.

There is one more thing about the story that moves me: the humility of the leprous man. He didn't stay away from Jesus; he was not passive. He did not demand that Jesus heal him. He simply believed Jesus could do it, he knelt before him in humility, and he asked.

This story moves me because I have broken places in my life that I would like Jesus to touch. Some of them are easy to see but others are not. Perhaps you have them as well. While it remains a mystery why some people are healed and others are not, this story shows me what God is like. He sees our brokenness. He cares. And he reaches out and touches us in our diseased state. God is not a distant, impersonal and aloof force in the universe. God is a person who reaches out to us in our need. He knows what we need and he is moved by it.

What comes to your mind when you read this description about Jesus?

Do you need Jesus to touch an area in your life? What is it?

Take a few minutes to talk with Jesus about it right now.

Prayer:

Jesus, when you were on this earth you saw people's need and your heart was moved by their suffering. Right now I bring myself to you like the man in Matthew 8. I cannot demand anything. I present my need before you. (Talk with Jesus now about your need even though he already knows.) Would you stretch out your hand and touch me in my need? I really need to know that you are here and that I am not alone in this. I trust your Word that says that in all things you work for the good of those who love you (Romans 8:28). I do love you and I ask you to have your way in my life. I rest in you now. Amen.

Receiving Jesus' Touch Through Others

You may decide to share your area that needs healing with your spiritual coach or your small group. We were not designed to suffer alone. Jesus designed us to be in community with others to "rejoice with those who rejoice" and to "mourn with those who mourn" (Romans 12:15), and to help "carry each other's burdens" (Galatians 6:2). Regardless of how we got to where we are, God will help us carry our burdens through his people. He may not remove our consequences. The law of sowing and reaping is part of the laws he set up in the universe. But he will help us. One way he helps us is through his people. It's humbling but it is right and it is good. I think you will like it as well.

ATTRIBUTE THREE · STEP TWO
RECOGNIZE JESUS' AUTHORITY

Scripture Memory:

⁷ "Ask and it ___ ___ ___ to you; seek and ___ ___ ___ ;
knock and the door ___ ___ ___ to you. ⁸ For everyone
who asks ___ ; the one who seeks ___ ; and to the one
who ___ , the door will be ___ ." ___ 7:7–8

⁷ *"Ask and it will be given to you; seek and you will find; knock
and the door will be opened to you. ⁸ For everyone who asks
receives; the one who seeks finds; and to the one who knocks, the
door will be opened." Matthew 7:7–8*

Read: Matthew 8:5–13

IN THIS STORY, a Roman military officer who was in charge
of a hundred men came to Jesus in Capernaum to let
Jesus know the officer's servant was paralyzed and in terrible
trouble. Jesus said to him, "Shall I come and heal him?" Several things about this surprise me. First, the man is not a Jew.
The average Jew hated the Roman occupation and wanted
nothing to do with any Roman citizens, especially the
soldiers. Somehow, the centurion knew Jesus was above all
that, that Jesus cared for everyone, even those who have
professions we disdain. Jesus obviously had a reputation
of caring for everyone. So, this man came to the one who
offered hope.

The second thing that surprises me is that Jesus offered to go and heal the man's servant without being asked. Jesus is proactive with his healing. When he hears a need, he responds. This surprises the centurion. He knows the social separation between Jews and Romans. Jews did not enter the homes of non-Jews because they thought it made them unclean. But Jesus was going to go anyway.

Why? Because people matter to God. God is not constrained by traditions and social rules that separate people from God. Aren't you glad of that? Jesus proactively goes to where the needs are.

Furthermore, the centurion is a man of great faith. The centurion tells Jesus he does not deserve to have Jesus come to his house. Instead, the centurion articulates his understanding of authority and then suggests that Jesus could just "say the word" and heal his servant without coming for a visit. The man's faith astonished Jesus and me as well. The man believed Jesus could heal from long distance.

This is exactly what Jesus did. "Jesus said to the centurion, 'Go! It will be done just as you believed it would.' And his servant was healed at that moment."

As you are learning about healing, you need to know that Jesus cares about people wherever they are found, that he is proactive, and that he responds to faith. The centurion put himself in a position to receive a miracle by believing that Jesus cared and that he could do it.

What comes to your mind as you think about this story?

....

How might a person put themselves in a position to receive a miracle? ....

....

As you read God's Word and observe how Jesus heals people, your faith in God will grow. Faith is simply believing that Jesus cares and that he can do it. It is confident trust.

Do you believe Jesus can heal now? Why or why not?

....

If you struggle with faith, you are not alone. You might be like Thomas, one of the twelve disciples, who struggled with his faith. After Jesus' resurrection, some of the disciples saw Jesus when Thomas was not around. When Thomas heard about it, he refused to believe. His words are recorded in John 20:25: "Unless I see the nail marks in his hands and put my finger where the nails were, and put my hand into his side, I will not believe." A week later, Jesus appeared to Thomas. He told Thomas to touch his hands and his side and then he said, "Stop doubting and believe." Jesus wasn't upset that Thomas struggled with his faith. He gave him objective data, but he also knew that Thomas needed to make an informed decision to believe.

You might be like the father who was described in Mark 9:14–32 whose son was being tormented by an evil spirit. When the father brought his son to Jesus, "Jesus said, 'Everything is possible for one who believes.' Immediately the boy's father exclaimed, 'I do believe; help me overcome my unbelief!'" (Mark 9:23–24). You may believe but you may also doubt. Bring all that to the Lord and ask him to help you with it.

Why not take some time right now to talk with the Lord about your needs. While you are at it, ask him for help with your faith as well. He can expand your capacity to have confident trust in him.

Prayer:
Heavenly Father, I am encouraged today that nothing can keep you from caring about my life. You have been reaching out to me my whole life. Even though I did not always respond, you continued to pursue me. I am so grateful for that. I believe you can do anything.

Increase my faith. Replace my doubts with faith. Show yourself to me in unmistakable ways and I will respond. (Take the time right now to present your needs to God. Ask him to heal or meet your need. Then, tell God you trust him with his decision.) Thank you for your unfailing love. I need you in my life today. Amen.

ATTRIBUTE THREE · STEP THREE
UNDERSTAND HEALING IS
GOD'S IDEA

Scripture Memory:

⁷ "Ask _____ _____ _____ _____ _____ to _____ ; seek _____ _____ _____ _____ ;
knock _____ _____ _____ _____ _____ _____ to _____ . ⁸ For _____
_____ asks _____ ; the one _____ _____ _____ ; _____ _____ the one
_____ _____ _____ , _____ _____ _____ _____ _____ ." _____ _____ :7–8

⁷ "Ask and it will be given to you; seek and you will find; knock and the door will be opened to you. ⁸ For everyone who asks receives; the one who seeks finds; and to the one who knocks, the door will be opened." Matthew 7:7–8

Read: Matthew 8:14–17

THE NEXT MIRACLE JESUS PERFORMED was to heal Peter's mother-in-law. (Peter's stock with his mother-in-law had to have gone up.) This healing was also a great move on Jesus' part because she was then able to wait on everyone. (Don't get upset. I'm just having some fun.) After that healing, many people were brought to Jesus to be delivered and healed. Don't miss the explanation in verse 17: "This was to fulfill what was spoken through the prophet Isaiah: 'He took up our infirmities and bore our diseases.'"

This is a direct quote of Isaiah 53. The book of Isaiah was written about seven hundred years before Jesus was born. Throughout the book there are hints of a leader who would come to change the course of history and bring peace. Isaiah 53:4–5 describes a suffering servant who would bring healing:

> Surely he took up our pain and bore our suffering, yet we considered him punished by God, stricken by him, and afflicted. But he was pierced for our transgressions, he was crushed for our iniquities; the punishment that brought us peace was on him, and by his wounds we are healed.

The early followers of Jesus were Jewish. They knew about this prophecy, and they rightly linked its fulfillment to Jesus. Isaiah 53 also describes the suffering servant pouring out his life unto death, bearing the sin of many, and interceding for people who are far from God. These were also fulfilled in Jesus.

I'm telling you all this because I want you to see that it is in the nature of God to heal and restore people. It is God's idea, not ours, that healing takes place. The One who spoke the world into existence can say the word and bring healing to your life.

God still heals bodies and does miracles, but the greatest miracle that will ever take place in your life is God healing your soul. Quoting from Isaiah 53:9, the Apostle Peter explains this in 1 Peter 2:22: "He committed no sin, and no deceit was found in his mouth." He then provided the following explanation in verses 23–25:

> When they hurled their insults at him, he did not retaliate; when he suffered, he made no threats. Instead, he entrusted himself to him who judges justly. "He himself bore our sins" in his body on the cross, so that we might die to sins and live for righteousness; "by his wounds you have been healed." For "you were like sheep going astray," but now you have returned to the Shepherd and Overseer of your souls.

We who were once far away from God, can now be close to God because Jesus bore our sins on the cross. Because Jesus did that, God can heal our souls. Why not take a few minutes right now to thank God that Jesus died for your sins and brought healing to your soul. Then, ask him to also heal your body...ask!

> ### *Prayer:*
> Heavenly Father, cause my faith to grow. I want to believe you can do anything. Thank you for healing my soul by sending Jesus to bear my sins on the cross. I know I cannot earn your love. Jesus has already earned it for me. I just accept what you did for me and I thank you. Thank you for making me new on the inside. Continue to heal me in every area of my life as well. (Take a few minutes now and tell the Lord about other areas of your life that need his healing touch. Pour out your heart to the Lord and trust him with the results.)

One final thought: healing may or may not come like you expect. But God does all things well. He is with you and you can trust him. He is always good and he is always loving.

ATTRIBUTE THREE · STEP FOUR
ASK IN FAITH

Scripture Memory:

7 "_____ _____ _____ given ___ ___; seek ____ ____ ____ ____ ;
____ ____ door ____ ___ ____ ____ ____ . 8 ____ everyone
____ ____ receives; ____ ___ ___ ____ finds; ____ ___ ___ ____ ____
knocks, ____ ___ ____ ____ ____." _____ 7: ___ – ___

7 *"Ask and it will be given to you; seek and you will find; knock and the door will be opened to you.* 8 *For everyone who asks receives; the one who seeks finds; and to the one who knocks, the door will be opened." Matthew 7:7–8*

Read: Matthew 9:1–8

I HOPE YOU HAVE SEEN BY NOW the connection between miracles and faith. Read Matthew 9:2 again closely. Whose faith moved Jesus to heal the man? ....

....

If you said the men who carried the paralytic to Jesus, you are correct. It always inspires me when I read about their faith. They carried their friend to Jesus because they believed Jesus could heal him. This has huge implications for followers of Jesus. You may have friends who are not sure if God can heal them, but you can bring them to Jesus anyway. As you listen and care for those around you, you will hear stories of heartache and pain, some physical and otherwise.

After you care for your friends and if you listen thoroughly to them, you may want to ask, "Do you mind if I pray for you?" Most friends will say, "That would be fine." Sometimes people will say, "No, thanks." Don't be discouraged by that. But if they do agree, find a quiet place off to the side or in a parking lot or wherever it seems appropriate and bring their need to Jesus. Sometimes you will not pray for them at that time but later. The point is that you will want to ask God on their behalf to heal them. Your prayer can be something like this, "Heavenly Father, I bring [say his name] to you right now. He needs you to bring healing in [name the area] of his life. You spoke and the world came into existence. You have intervened many times and changed the course of history. I believe you can do it again. I ask You now to just say the word and heal [name]. We promise to give you all the honor and the glory for the healing. In Jesus' name we pray, amen." If you begin to ask God for healing, you will begin to see his supernatural intervention in your life and in the lives of those around you. It's pretty cool that God responds to our asking.

I want you to make another observation about this particular story. What did Jesus say after he saw their faith?

Does his response surprise you? I was expecting him to say, "Rise up and walk" but he says instead, "Take heart, son; your sins are forgiven." The rest of the story explains why Jesus did that. He wanted everyone to know that he can not only heal our bodies, he can also heal souls. He did say, "Get up, take your mat and go home." And the man did that and went home. The people praised God because of what Jesus did.

It is an awesome thing that Jesus is able to heal the whole person. God is changing your life, and he will change the lives of anyone who asks. Ultimately and in God's timing, we are all going to die a physical death. But if Jesus heals our souls by forgiving our sins, we will live forever with God. I love the verse in 1 John 1:9, "If we confess our sins, he is faithful and just and will forgive us our sins and purify us from all unrighteousness."

Why not take a few minutes right now to thank God for healing your soul by forgiving your sins. Take a few minutes also to begin praying for the needs of your friends. What a wonderful privilege it is to present your friends' needs to the one who holds the whole world in his hands. I won't write out a prayer for you this time. Just use your own words to communicate with God.

ATTRIBUTE THREE · STEP FIVE
GIVE IT AWAY

Scripture Memory:

7 "_____ ___ __ ____ __ ____ __ ___; _____ ___ ___ ____ ___;
_____ ___ _____ ____ ___ __ ____ __ ___. 8 __ ____
_____ ___ _____; ___ ___ ___ ____; ___ __ ___ ___ ____
_____ , ___ ___ ___ _____ ." _____ __:_ – __

7 "*Ask and it will be given to you; seek and you will find; knock and the door will be opened to you.* 8 *For everyone who asks receives; the one who seeks finds; and to the one who knocks, the door will be opened.*" Matthew 7:7–8

Read: Matthew 10:1–8

I HAVE OFTEN WONDERED HOW IT MUST HAVE FELT to be a follower of Jesus in person. It would have been amazing to see him perform miracles and to hear him speak. When you read this passage you see his intent that his followers would do as he did: preach the nearness of God's kingdom and perform miracles (healing, cleansing, driving out demons, et cetera). How would you have felt if Jesus said to you, "I give you authority to drive out evil spirits and to heal every disease and sickness"? ....

....

I would have felt inadequate, excited, humbled, and hopeful at the same time. The most encouraging words to me

98

are found in Matthew 10:8, "Freely you have received, freely give." Jesus expects us to give away what he has given to us. Gifts that we receive are to be used, not hoarded.

There are plenty of examples in the New Testament of how the disciples did heal people with the power of the Holy Spirit. One example is found in Acts 3. Read Acts 3:1–10. What stands out to you about this story?

Praying for people to be healed is only giving away what God gives you. Over the years I (Bryan) have been blessed to witness God provide miracles of healing for numbers of people. One that stands out in my mind is my sister-in-law Ronda and her husband Dave. They had experienced some difficulty in having children early in their marriage. Ronda's condition involved thinning along the wall of the uterus, which made it difficult for the fertilized egg to remain attached and grow. After much prayer and medical intervention, Ronda was able to conceive and gave birth to their first child, Leah. God gave Dave and Ronda the desire to have another child and knowing what they went through to have Leah, they decided not to enlist the help of the fertility specialist again. After several years of being poked and probed, taking medications and enduring procedures, they decided this time to release the entire situation to God.

They were trusting God for healing and to conceive naturally, or perhaps I should say supernaturally. At the end of a weekend service, Ronda came to the altar. I remember her praying fervently with tears, and I believed with her that she would conceive a child with God's help. It was only a short time after that encounter that I had a dream where I clearly saw Ronda late in pregnancy full of joy and excitement. I struggled with telling her this story as I have always been cautious of my approach in these situations, but I eventually shared my dream with Ronda and told her that I strongly believed that God would answer our prayers. A few weeks later Ronda and Dave stopped by our house to share some wonderful news. God had intervened supernaturally; Ronda was pregnant. Nine months later on their ten-year wedding anniversary, Dave and Ronda held in their arms a healthy baby boy named Jacob. God answers prayers. Begin to ask God to heal yourself and others. Ask and believe.

About five years after I (Daniel) was out of college, I happened to see a friend of mine. As we shared what life was like now that we were out of college, he began to pour out his heart about wanting a child. He and his wife had been trying for a long time but with no results. As he talked, I felt my heart welling up with compassion for them at a level I had rarely felt for anyone. When we got done, I asked him if I could pray for them. We prayed together, and shortly after that his wife was able to get pregnant. Some time later another friend had a similar story. Since God had done it before, I told that person the story. We prayed and my friends who had been trying for about thirteen years were able to conceive a child. Since that time, I have seen quite a few people conceive who before weren't able. One couple, Matthew and Jennifer Olson, were unable to conceive their first child, Hannah, without great effort: the help of multiple fertility specialists, in three different states and various fertility drugs over the course of ten years. When they heard about these miracles, they asked for prayer. We prayed and they were able to conceive their second child, Jonathan, without any medical intervention. I am telling you this not so you can be wowed at this gift, but so you will begin to ask God to heal you and others. Ask.

Read 1 Corinthians 12:4–11. It is really important to remember that God is always the hero. He just lets us be a part of the miracle. Reread 1 Corinthians 12:6. Who is it who works gifts in all men? ....

That's right! It's God and not us. We are just instruments through whom God works. It amazes me that God includes us in his work. He could just do it on his own but he lets us be part of it. That amazes me! I also want you to notice 1 Corinthians 12:9. Notice that "gifts" is plural. In other words, there is more than one gift of healing. God can do anything he wants through any of us. If the Spirit of God is in you, then the same God who spoke the world into existence can do great things through you. He is the same God. Every believer has been given the authority to pray for those who are sick or afflicted. With that being said, I have also observed that God tends to use some people more in one area of healing and other people in other areas.

We need to address one last thing before we move on: the question, "Why does God heal one thing and not another?" Whole books are written on this subject.[1] I (Bryan) already mentioned that God healed my right eye but not my left eye. Even though I have prayed many, many times for healing, God did not heal it. I (Daniel) told how God healed me of a broken arm and a hernia, but God did not heal my knee. I had a painful sports injury with torn ligaments and cartilage. I also struggle from time to time with depression. It seems to be a genetic thing. Both my parents and many of my extended family members struggle with this as well. There are some who say we are not healed because of lack of faith. There is certainly a link between lack of faith and lack of healing. Matthew 13:58 describes what happened when Jesus went to his hometown, "And he did not do many miracles there because of their lack of faith." We need to be careful not to judge, however, because sometimes people have faith but God chooses not to heal. When this happens, one thing is certain. God's character never changes. Ten times in the Bible God is described as a "compassionate and gracious God, slow to anger and abounding in love" (Exodus 34:6;

2 Chronicles 30:9; Nehemiah 9:17; Psalms 86:15, 103:8, 111:4, 112:4, 145:8; Joel 2:13; Jonah 4:2). In other words, God's choice to heal one and not another is not based on his love and compassion for an individual. God is always loving and he always cares for you. When he chooses not to heal, I have two recommendations. First, trust him. Don't freak out and turn your back on him in anger. He is your best friend. Even if you turn your back on him, he will never turn his back on you. He loves you and you can trust him. Second, look for the good in the situation. You may not see it right away, perhaps never, but look for it anyway. I have clung to the truth of Romans 8:28 when life doesn't make sense: "And we know that in all things God works for the good of those who love him, who have been called according to his purpose." It doesn't say that "all things are good." It says that "in all things God works for the good of those who love him." So, ask God for healing; believe that he can heal; experience healing, and trust him when he chooses to not heal. This was a longer section today, but I want to pray for you.

Prayer:

Heavenly Father, thank you for your kindness in our lives. I am encouraged today, even while I am writing this, that your character never changes, that you are a gracious and compassionate God, slow to anger and abounding in love. We have been through a lot together, and you have always been kind to me. Even when you have allowed me to go through painful things, both physically and emotionally, you have been there for me. Help my friends who are reading this book to learn that about you as well. Help them to cling to you in times of joy and sorrow, when you heal and when you choose to do things differently from what we ask. Teach my friends to rejoice in you at all times and to find your corresponding peace because of it (Philippians 4:4–7). We need you at every turn in our lives. Give my friends faith to believe you are "able to do immeasurably more than all we ask or imagine, according to [your] power that is at work within us, to [you] be glory in the church and in Christ Jesus throughout all generations, for ever and ever! Amen" (Ephesians 3:20–21).

ATTRIBUTE THREE
DECISIONS

ATTRIBUTE FOUR

• • •

LEARN TO INFLUENCE

ATTRIBUTE FOUR
INTRODUCTION
LEARN TO INFLUENCE

(DANIEL) GREW UP IN A HOME AND A CHURCH that believed your life should radically change when you come to Christ. When Jesus Christ comes into your life, he makes you a new person. The old has gone; the new has come. I believe that. When I was growing up, I saw some people's lives change but never on the scale and magnitude of what I read about in the book of Acts.

As I read and reread the Gospels and Acts, three things stood out to me about influencing people for Christ. First, followers of Jesus are called to attract people to him. Jesus told his followers they are to be the salt of the earth and the light of the world (Matthew 5:13–16). Salt on food makes you want to come back for more. Light shows you the right path. Jesus embodied this. His teaching style was attractive. His personality was magnetic. The miracles he did and the way he cared for his disciples attracted people, causing them to want to follow him. He was "attractional."

Second, we need the empowerment of the Holy Spirit to be effective witnesses for Christ. After Jesus resurrected from the dead and before he ascended into heaven, Jesus told his disciples to wait until they had been empowered by the Holy Spirit (Acts 1:8). Jesus had given his followers an impossible task, "Make disciples of all nations" (Matthew 28:18–20). Think about it for a minute. There were no planes, trains, automobiles, mass mailing systems, televisions, telephones, or Internet. All they had was a changed life and a promise that when the Holy Spirit came on them, they would have power to witness effectively. At a large Jewish celebration called Pentecost just fifty days after Jesus' resurrection, it happened. The early followers of Jesus were in prayer, waiting for the empowerment of the Holy Spirit, when a supernatural wind filled the place where they were sitting. People saw something that looked like tongues of fire that separated and rested on everyone present. Every follower of Christ present began to speak in languages they had never learned.[1] People in the street heard what was happening and were surprised to hear someone in Jerusalem praising God in their native language when their native language was not the language spoken in Jerusalem. In the middle of that scene, Peter stood to address the growing crowd. Just fifty days prior, Peter denied being a follower of Jesus at nighttime to a servant girl. Yet in this story, he is able to stand before a crowd of thousands to challenge them to a decision to follow Jesus. That can happen when the Holy Spirit empowers a person. It can happen to you. About three thousand people made commitments to follow Christ that day and were baptized. That's an effective day.

Third, sharing Christ is personal. One exciting thing I discovered in my study was there are different styles for sharing your faith that are modeled in the New Testament: confrontational, intellectual, testimonial, relational, invitational, and serving. Your style of sharing Christ will look different from others. Each day we will explore a different style and then ask God to empower us by his Holy Spirit to share Christ effectively.

Take some time right now to ask God to empower you with the Holy Spirit like he did with the early followers of Jesus so you can be the most effective witness you can be. It is not something you should fear. Jesus said, "If you then, though you are evil, know how to give good gifts to your children, how much more will your Father in heaven give the

Holy Spirit to those who ask him!" (Luke 11:13).

Do not be surprised if the Holy Spirit enables you to speak in a language you have never learned. It is not uncommon at all. In fact, it is normal and can be expected. If this whole thing is new to you or if you are uncomfortable about it, make it a matter of prayer. It should not produce anxiety in you. It is a good thing from God. He will lead you as you seek him. I have personally experienced this, and it is part of my daily prayer life with God. Feel free to talk with your spiritual coach if you have questions.

Prayer:

Heavenly Father, I worship you today. There is none like you. You reached out to me, accepted me, forgave me, and you are changing my life. I ask you to empower me by your Holy Spirit today like you did your early followers. Completely baptize me in the Holy Spirit. Enable me to praise you beyond my own words and understanding. I want and need your power to be the witness you are calling me to be. There are people all around me who are hungry for you. Give me the ability to share Christ with them effectively. I wait for you now to empower me. (I encourage you to be responsive now to the work of the Holy Spirit in your life. If he gives you words to pray, pray them. If he gives you words that are beyond your understanding that sound like another language, say them. It is the Holy Spirit praying through you. When the Holy Spirit enables you to pray, it is a beautiful thing.)

ATTRIBUTE FOUR · STEP ONE
INVITE PEOPLE

Scripture Memory (new):

¹⁸ Then Jesus came to them and said, "All authority in heaven and on earth has been given to me. ¹⁹ Therefore go and make disciples of all nations, baptizing them in the name of the Father and of the Son and of the Holy Spirit, ²⁰ and teaching them to obey everything I have commanded you. And surely I am with you always, to the very end of the age." Matthew 28:18–20

Scripture Memory (review):   Matthew 4:19
    Matthew 11:28–30   Matthew 7:24–25
    Matthew 7:7–8

Take the Evangelism Styles Questionnaire on page 224.

Read: John 1:40–46

ONE OF THE MOST EXCITING THINGS you will ever do is bring a friend to Jesus. The excitement is not just yours. Jesus said, "There is rejoicing in the presence of the angels of God over one sinner who repents" (Luke 15:10). But how do you do that?

The hard times we go through give us the opportunity to share our story and naturally invite people to church. When you share your story, God can use that to bring healing. I (Bryan) have seen it work powerfully as I have had more chances to meet people who are going through difficulties than ever before. As a result of what I have been through, people ask how I'm able to deal with all that's happened to me and still remain joyful. That is the perfect open door to share the story of God's work in my life. I was in rehab learning how to use my new prosthetic leg right before Christmas, and I invited my entire floor to our Christmas Eve services! And the miracle is many of them came and heard about God's love and grace for the very first time.

One of the most logical ways to bring people to Christ is to literally bring people to events where they can meet Christ, to church services, concerts, parties, et cetera. Studies show that people are most likely to follow Christ because of the influence of a friend or family member.[1] This is especially significant for parents with children, since 64 percent of people who follow Jesus said they made the decision before they were age 18.[2]

This is exactly what you see when Andrew met Jesus. John 1:41–42 reads, "The first thing Andrew did was to find his brother Simon and tell him, 'We have found the Messiah' (that is, the Christ). And he brought him to Jesus." The Apostle Peter came to Jesus because his brother brought him.

Do you have some friends or family members you would like to introduce to Jesus?

Is that something you would like to do?

Who would you like to invite first?

What are some logical ways you can invite someone to meet Jesus?

At our churches we work at creating friendly, warm, caring environments for our church members, regular attendees, and guests. Throughout your entire worship experience, you should feel a sense of being a part of a family. As you drive into the parking lot, you will be welcomed by a friendly parking attendant followed by a warm greeting as you walk through the front door. Whether you choose to partake of the good food we offer or immediately enter a worship area, a warm smile and greeting will be waiting for you. We provide helpful information via our website, weekly handouts, and announcements prior to the sermon. We use a teaching style that everyone can embrace and understand. God wants his people welcomed in his house. We are passionate about maintaining environments where people feel drawn to become fully devoted followers of Jesus Christ. We give people non-threatening opportunities to make a commitment to Christ because we want everyone to know Jesus. We hope you feel comfortable bringing your friends to your church as part of how you introduce your friends to Christ.[3]

Do you feel free to invite your friends and family to your church? Why or why not?

What could your church do to make the gathering a better place to bring your friends and family?

There are other opportunities for inviting guests to church. Special services like child dedication, baptism, Easter, and Christmas provide a great opening to invite friends and family. May I suggest a few more: a rainy day, a sunny day, a beautiful autumn morning, a humid summer Saturday evening? Any day is a good day to invite a guest to church. No matter the season or the weather, God will be there.

There are some practical steps you can take to start bringing your friends to Christ. First, make a list of your friends and family members who could benefit from a relationship with Jesus. There are four logical categories of people who are close to you. Write down who comes to your mind that you might want to introduce to Jesus:

- Friends
- Family Members
- Co-workers
- Neighbors

Second, continue to pray for them. Jesus said in John 6:44, "No one can come to me unless the Father who sent me draws them." No one loses their free will to accept or reject Christ, but you can pray for each person in the following ways:

+ Present the person to God by name as someone for whom he died.

+ Ask God to pull this person to himself, to open her eyes to the emptiness of life without him.

+ Ask God to help her see her need for forgiveness and to remove any confusion about God and the good life he offers.

+ Ask God to help her understand the meaning and the importance of Christ's finished work on the cross.

+ Ask God to open her heart to his love and truth.
You can also pray for yourself in the following ways:

+ Ask God to help you live a consistent and attractive Christian life.

+ Ask God to help you be authentic and honest as you deal with life's ups and downs.

+ Ask God to give you wisdom to know how to approach the relationship.

+ Ask God to grant you appropriate boldness and courage to communicate his love effectively.

+ Ask God to expand your knowledge so you will be ready to define and communicate God's message clearly.

+ Ask God to use you to lead this person into a relationship with Christ.

Prayer:

(Take a few minutes right now to pray for the people on your list using the suggestions above to guide you.)

ATTRIBUTE FOUR · STEP TWO
SHARE YOUR STORY

Scripture Memory:

¹⁸ Then _____ came to them and _____, "All authority in _____ and on earth ___ ___ _____to me. ¹⁹ _____ go and _____ disciples of all nations, baptizing _____ in the name of the_____ and of the ___ and of the Holy _____, ²⁰ and teaching them to _____ everything I have commanded you. And _____ I am with you always, to the ____ end of the age." _____ 28:18–20

¹⁸ Then Jesus came to them and said, "All authority in heaven and on earth has been given to me. ¹⁹ Therefore go and make disciples of all nations, baptizing them in the name of the Father and of the Son and of the Holy Spirit, ²⁰ and teaching them to obey everything I have commanded you. And surely I am with you always, to the very end of the age."
Matthew 28:18–20

Read: John 9:1–25

EVERYONE'S STORY WITH JESUS IS DIFFERENT. As you look back on your life, you will probably see how God has been reaching out to you through circumstances, people, and experiences. Perhaps a friend or co-worker lived a different lifestyle that stood out to you and attracted you to Christ. Perhaps a friend or a family member showed you kindness or support during an important season in your life. While we all have the same need for forgiveness and relationship with God through Jesus, how someone becomes a follower of Christ is always unique.

There are at least four reasons why it is important for you to tell your story. First, it helps people around you know why your life is changing. Second, it brings honor to God. Although you are an important person in your story, God is really the hero. Only God can change a life. Third, it gives people hope that God can change their lives as well. Fourth, it is difficult for anyone to argue with your experience. While you may not have all the answers to their questions, you can share what you know, how Jesus is changing your life.

Based on John 9:1–2, what do you think the man's life was like before he met Jesus?

How did Jesus change his life?

The people who were questioning this man were well educated and powerful. Why was his story so powerful to them even though he was neither educated nor powerful?

Read John 9:35–38. How did this man become a believer in Jesus?

What happened after the man believed?

Take a few minutes now and write out your story using the following questions to guide you.

Writing Your Story

- Where were you spiritually before receiving Christ?

- How did that affect you—your feelings, attitudes, actions, and relationships?

- What caused you to begin considering Christ as a solution to your needs?

- What realization did you come to that finally motivated you to receive Christ?

- What did you do specifically to receive Christ?

- How has your life begun to change since you trusted Christ?

- What other benefits have you experienced since becoming a follower of Christ?

- Is there a passage of Scripture that means a lot to you now that you are a follower of Christ?

We have a few suggestions. First, share your story with your spiritual coach. It will be good practice even though you may have already told him or her. Second, take the time to write out your story in its entirety. If you have a computer, type it up. We invite you to send it to us at this e-mail address: **stories@learningtofollow.net.** We really enjoy hearing how God changes people's lives. Let us know if you are comfortable with us sharing it with others. We may post it on the website so people can hear how God is changing lives. Third, practice telling your story in private. Say it again and again until you are comfortable sharing it. Fourth, reduce your story. Most people will listen for about three minutes without feeling imposed upon. Less is best. Fifth, ask a friend or family member if you can share your story with him. When you are done, thank him for listening. Ask him what he thinks of your story. Tell him that if he ever wants to share his spiritual journey, you would enjoy hearing it.

Prayer:

Thank you, Heavenly Father, for changing my life. I know you are going to continue to change me as well. I lift my friends and family up to you right now. (Present them by name to God now.) Draw them to yourself. Use circumstances and situations to help them realize you love them and have a purpose for their lives. Help me to be an accurate witness of how you can change a life. I know I cannot do that on my own. Use me to bring people to you. Amen.

ATTRIBUTE FOUR · STEP THREE
BE A GENUINE FRIEND

Scripture Memory:

¹⁸ Then _____ came to _____ and _____, "All _____ in _____ and on _____ has _____ given to me. ¹⁹ _____ go and _____ of all _____, baptizing _____ in the _____ of the _____ and of the _____ and of the _____ _____, ²⁰ and teaching _____ to _____ everything I have _____ you. And _____ I am _____ you _____, to the _____ end of the _____." Matthew _____ :18–20

¹⁸ *Then Jesus came to them and said, "All authority in heaven and on earth has been given to me.* ¹⁹ *Therefore go and make disciples of all nations, baptizing them in the name of the Father and of the Son and of the Holy Spirit,* ²⁰ *and teaching them to obey everything I have commanded you. And surely I am with you always, to the very end of the age."* *Matthew 28:18–20*

Read: Luke 5:27–30

A s I (Daniel) started to try to engage my friends in spiritual conversations, I realized I didn't know how to relate to them. I was raised to "come out from among them, and be ye separate" (2 Corinthians 6:17 KJV). I was so culturally separate that I often did not know what people were talking about. As I read the Gospels, I realized I needed to adopt the mindset of a missionary. I needed to learn to communicate

Christ in an understandable way with my potential friends. A missionary often learns a new language and culture to communicate effectively. I started studying my culture, listening to people and learning how they thought. I also began to prayerfully and carefully immerse myself in the culture without giving up my morals.

As I read the New Testament, I was encouraged by what I saw in Jesus. He was comfortable interacting with people from a variety of backgrounds and life situations. His primary mode was to love and accept people. He did not lower his standard of righteousness. He was with people where they were and they were attracted to his life. As I attempted to allow Christ to do this through me, I began to see my friends come to Christ, not in great numbers but one at a time. I discovered that people are much more open to Christ than I had expected. Many people know something is missing in their lives but they just don't know what it is. Unfortunately, many followers of Christ stay away from people with pre-Christian lifestyles. As a result, they are unable to have the impact Jesus said we should have. It is tough to lead people to Christ if you are not their friend.

I want you to think for a minute about your best friend. What is he or she like? (If you don't have a best friend, think for a minute about the characteristics you would like to have in a friend.)

The book of Proverbs describes a good friend as one who has the following characteristics:

- ◆ Faithful and consistent (Proverbs 17:17)
- ◆ Keeps secrets (Proverbs 11:13, 25:9–10)
- ◆ Available and dependable (Proverbs 27:10, 18:24, 20:6, 25:19)
- ◆ Has gracious speech (Proverbs 22:11)

- Not easily annoyed but patient (Proverbs 12:16)
- One who understands you (Proverbs 20:5)
- One who helps you become a wiser person (Proverbs 27:17, 13:20)
- Generous (Proverbs 19:6, 11:25, 18:16, 19:6, 22:9)
- Sensitive to your feelings (Proverbs 25:20)
- A friend with your parents (Proverbs 27:10)
- Able to accept advice and a rebuke (Proverbs 13:10, 27:6)
- Pleasant to be around (Proverbs 27:9)

I don't know anyone who doesn't want a friend with the characteristics mentioned above. Which of these characteristics does your best friend have?

Which characteristics would you like to see more of in your life?

What kind of a friend was Levi according to Luke 5?

What does it tell you about Jesus that Levi was comfortable inviting Jesus to a banquet with his "sinner" friends?

What do you think it meant that Jesus was a friend of sinners? (Luke 7:34)

Are you a friend of sinners? How so?

Friendship is often enjoying something with another person. What are some things you like to do for fun that you could do with someone who hasn't yet made a commitment to Christ?

Do you know anyone with whom you can enjoy that fun thing who needs Jesus?

A good friend listens to you. Unfortunately, most of us are not good listeners. We all like to talk about ourselves and our ideas. However, as you are allowing Christ to change you, he is going to show you how to become more others-centered rather than self-centered. You will start to care more about the other person's story rather than the story you want to tell. I encourage you to practice listening to others by doing the following:

→ When someone starts sharing something with you, stop and focus on her. Maintain comfortable eye contact. Face the person if it is appropriate. Let her know by your actions that what she is talking about is important to you.

→ Summarize her content and feelings. You may use a phrase like, "Let me see if I understand you. Am I correct in saying…" Or, "It sounds like you were stressed at work today." If she says, "Well, that's really not it," then you didn't hear her correctly. Try again.

→ Discipline yourself to focus on the person and her story rather than thinking about what you are going to say and a story you want to tell.

→ Don't interrupt or complete the person's sentences.

→ Don't be afraid of a few seconds of silence. Sometimes people need to think before they start talking again. Be patient.

→ Don't be quick to give advice. Listen and care about the person. People are turned off by pushy and arrogant people. Giving a quick answer can feel like both.

Many people are open to Christ when they go through a crisis of some sort. If you have been a good friend before the crisis, your friend will trust you in a crisis. Offer to pray for your friend and be open to sharing Christ especially at that time.

Prayer:

Take a few minutes to ask God to help you be a better friend. Tell God aspects of friendship with which you need him to help you. Ask God to show you with whom you can spend time as a friend.

ATTRIBUTE FOUR · STEP FOUR
SPEAK DIRECTLY

Scripture Memory:

[18] Then _____ came to _____ and _____, "All _____ in _____ and on _____ _____ _____ _____ to me. [19] _____ go and _____ _____ of all _____, baptizing _____ in the _____ of the_____ and of the_____ and of the_____ _____, [20] and teaching _____ to _____ everything I have _____ you. And _____ I am _____ you _____, to the _____ end of the _____." Matthew 28: ___–

[18] *Then Jesus came to them and said, "All authority in heaven and on earth has been given to me.* [19] *Therefore go and make disciples of all nations, baptizing them in the name of the Father and of the Son and of the Holy Spirit,* [20] *and teaching them to obey everything I have commanded you. And surely I am with you always, to the very end of the age."*
Matthew 28:18–20

Read: Acts 2:1–41; 8:4–8, 26–40

WHAT COMES TO YOUR MIND when you think of the word "evangelist"? If you are like many others, you think of people like Billy Graham in front of stadiums of people. Some of us think of televangelists or street preachers. Millions of people in the United States and around the world have decided to follow Christ because of the gifted ministry of Billy Graham and others who speak directly about the love of God. This is somewhat similar to what Peter did on the day of Pentecost. Do not think, however, that the direct approach to sharing Christ has to be done by a trained professional in a stadium. It can be an individual speaking directly about Christ to a person in private like Phillip did with the Ethiopian eunuch. The direct approach works for some because they have not yet accepted Christ and are ready to respond. They just need an opportunity.

Every follower of Christ needs to learn how to share the message of Christ directly. While the direct approach may not be your primary mode, you need to be prepared to help people find Christ if they are ready.

Be prepared to share your story openly. I (Bryan) have found that since my accident, the more willing I am to talk honestly about my struggles and personal journey, the more people feel comfortable and safe sharing their own story. I have also found I am even more bold in speaking directly to people about the need to get right with God before it's too late.

The Gospel message is simple. Look up each passage of Scripture below and memorize the message. You may want to make a copy of it and put it in your Bible.

+ God loves you and has a wonderful plan for your life (1 John 4:16).

+ God is holy (1 Peter 1:16) and just (2 Thessalonians 1:6).

+ We were created holy but we became sinful (Romans 3:23).

+ Because of our sin, we deserve death (Romans 6:23).

+ It is only by God's gift of grace that we are able to be saved (Ephesians 2:8–9).

→ Jesus who was fully God became a man (John 1:1, 14), died in our place (1 Peter 3:18; 2 Corinthians 5:21), and offers forgiveness as a gift (Romans 6:23).

→ You must respond (John 1:12) by asking Christ to be your leader and forgiver (1 John 1:9, 1 Peter 3:15).

→ When you do that, the Holy Spirit will transform your life (2 Corinthians 5:17; 1 Corinthians 6:19-20).

Prayer:

Heavenly Father, I pray for boldness to share the message of Christ with people who do not yet know you. You have been good to me, and I want others to know about you. Help me to be aware of people around me who are open to Christ. Give me the courage to share with them. Give me an opportunity today to talk with someone about who you are and the difference you can make in our lives. Amen.

ATTRIBUTE FOUR · STEP FIVE
SERVE PEOPLE

Scripture Memory:

¹⁸ _____ _____ , " _____
_____ . ¹⁹ _____
_____ , _____ _____
_____ , _____ _____
_____ , ²⁰ _____ _____
_____ . _____ _____ ,
_____ . " _____ ___ : ___ — ___

¹⁸ Then Jesus came to them and said, "All authority in heaven and on earth has been given to me. ¹⁹ Therefore go and make disciples of all nations, baptizing them in the name of the Father and of the Son and of the Holy Spirit, ²⁰ and teaching them to obey everything I have commanded you. And surely I am with you always, to the very end of the age."
Matthew 28:18–20

Read: John 13:1–17, 34–35; Acts 9

MOST OF US CAN REMEMBER SOMEONE who has served us at a particular season in our lives when we needed help. When I (Bryan) reflect on those who poured into my life, the person who comes to mind is my mother. She is a caring person who loves God and truly enjoys serving people. Numerous people have been on the receiving end of her encouraging words, heartfelt prayers, and wonderfully baked desserts. My father, sister, and I have all enjoyed the fruits of my mother's love and devotion. I found out how much I appreciated my mom when I left home for the first time for spring training. Fast food, pink socks, and dirty apartments; it didn't take long to realize how much I had been loved and served over the years.

However, all of the physical needs that my mom provided for me over the years cannot compare with the spiritual care she gave me when I was facing the most difficult season of my life. My mom was by my side, reading the Word and praying for me continuously while I was fighting for my life in the hospital. But she wasn't just praying for me. She was praying for all the families with loved ones in the ICU at the same time I was there. In fact, the hospital staff commented that things were just "different" while my mom was around. Her amazing faith and deep concern for others is just an inspiration. After I returned home from my fifty-one days in the hospital, my mom wrote personal thank you notes to everyone who was involved in my care—the first responders, medical workers, community members, and other churches who all were integral to my story. The impact she has had on my life and the life of my family is enormous. Because of her service, I want to serve others as well.

When I (Daniel) was twenty-three years old, I had to have reconstructive knee surgery because of an injury I had sustained while playing basketball a few years prior. A few weeks after the surgery, Amy (my wife) and I found out we were going to have to move. I was on crutches at the time and was wondering how we would get our furniture moved into our new place since both of our families were out of state. We had just started attending a new church so we did not have any close friends yet. Amy and I also started attending a small group with some friends at Gordon-Conwell Theological Seminary. When they heard about our situation, they did not ask if we needed any help. They said, "We'll be at your house on Saturday morning to move you." And they were. They arrived early and worked hard until everything we owned was moved into the new place. They even helped us on the other end to set everything up. And they had a boatload of fun while they did it. It was one of the nicest gifts I have ever received. As I am writing this, I am still grateful for those friends: Dave and Lisa Helm, Jimmy and Sally Dodd, Tim and Sally Kirk. Because of their service, I want to help everyone who moves. Being served can have that effect on people.

That's exactly what Jesus did for his disciples and the people around them. When he saw someone in need he served them. The key theme of the Gospel of Mark summarizes this aspect about Jesus: "For even the Son of Man did not come to be served, but to serve, and to give his life as a ransom for many" (Mark 10:45). One of the marks of followers of Christ is their service to others.

One of the most moving stories in the Bible that illustrates this aspect of Jesus is found in John 13:1–17. The disciples and Jesus arrived in Jerusalem for the Passover, a massive Jewish celebration that reminded the Jews how God miraculously brought them out of slavery in Egypt. Jesus and the disciples either borrowed or rented a room where they could have their Passover meal. Normally a servant would be present to wash people's feet as they came into the house, but none was present that day. Jesus surprised everyone by taking on the role of a servant and washing all the disciples' feet. Think about it for a minute. The Son of God, the one who spoke the world into existence, the one who would save the world, got down on his knees and washed the dirty feet of his disciples. By doing this, he demonstrated that no act of service was too low for him or us. John records Jesus teaching his disciples about this in John 13:14–17:

> Now that I, your Lord and Teacher, have washed your feet, you
> also should wash one another's feet. I have set you an example

that you should do as I have done for you. Very truly I tell you, no servant is greater than his master, nor is a messenger greater than the one who sent him. Now that you know these things, you will be blessed if you do them.

What kinds of things come to your mind when you think about the call to serve people?..

Who around you needs to be served right now? What are their needs?...

Do you have any ideas about how you or others could serve others?...

What part of serving will be a challenge for you?.................

....

There are a number of ways you can serve your church. There are plenty of opportunities: guest services, building and grounds, general office help, and many other ministries. You can also serve your neighbors. You could serve your family. What are their needs? What do you have to give?

When you serve, you are going to feel God's joy because that's how he designed us. Will you make a decision today to make your life about serving others?

Prayer:

Jesus, it humbles me that you came to serve people. You are the Creator of the universe. You hold everything in your hand. You have all power and authority and yet you stoop down to wash feet, my dirty feet and my dirty heart. You came to this earth to forgive me of my sin, to show me how to have an abundant life, and to show me how I could be with you forever. Your serving me in those ways humbles me. It brings focus to my life, why I am here. It's not naturally in me to make my life about others. Even when I am serving others, it is often about me, wanting people to affirm me or thank me or appreciate me. I really need your help to learn how to serve in a way that is about you and the people I am serving. Teach me how to do that. Grow a servant's heart in me. Have your way in and through my life. Amen.

ATTRIBUTE FOUR · STEP SIX
MAKE SENSE

Scripture Memory:

18 _____, " _____ _____
_____ . 19 _____
_____, _____ _____ _____
_____ _____ _____
_____, 20 _____
_____ . _____ _____, ___ ___
_____ _____ ___ . " _____ ___ : ___ —

18 Then Jesus came to them and said, "All authority in heaven and on earth has been given to me. 19 Therefore go and make disciples of all nations, baptizing them in the name of the Father and of the Son and of the Holy Spirit, 20 and teaching them to obey everything I have commanded you. And surely I am with you always, to the very end of the age."
Matthew 28:18–20

Read: Acts 17:16–34

MANY CHRISTIANS HAVE BEEN LED TO BELIEVE that asking questions about the Bible or matters of faith equates to doubt or unbelief. Nothing could be further from the truth. A reason that many Christ followers do not share their faith with their family and friends more regularly is fear of being asked questions that they cannot answer. Our Scripture memory verse includes the phrases "making disciples" and "teaching them to obey." Would it be possible to make disciples and teach others without allowing questioning for clarification? I really don't think so. Sincere faith does not need be fearful of deep questioning as it will be answered by the truth of God's Word.

I (Daniel) have always been an inquisitive person. Sometimes it is a blessing and sometimes it is a curse. In my teen years I went to an important person in my life with two major questions. First, I wanted to know why my mother was not emotionally healthy. I loved my mother, but her behavior made her difficult to be around. We did not know she was bipolar until many years later, but we knew something was not right. Her view of spirituality and her insecurity did not allow her to acknowledge that she had a problem. I wanted to know where God was in our situation. She seemed to love God but had major abnormalities when it came to relating to people. Why? Second, I wanted to know how we know the Bible is accurate. The person to whom I brought these questions did not respond to my questions but instead asked me what was wrong with me that I had those kinds of questions. The person said I needed to honor my mother and believe the Bible. He said I obviously had rebellion problems and needed to get right with God. The person was probably right on both accounts, but I still had my questions. I left that meeting, unfortunately, believing there were no answers to my questions. When I went into the meeting, my real question was whether or not God existed. When I left the meeting, I felt like I had no option but to stop believing. I could not make myself believe, and I could not deny the questions. I gradually slipped into agnosticism after that. Agnostics do not believe in God but they are not absolutely sure. For a couple of years, I tried to believe but found myself not believing most of the time. The worst part was that I did not feel I could talk with anyone about this. I had been led to believe it was wrong to ask questions. Why didn't I just believe and go along with what others said I should believe? I did not know why belief was so difficult for me.

In February of 1983, I (Bryan) arrived in Sarasota, Florida, for my first full spring training. I roomed with a pitcher who was a mature and deeply spiritual born-again Christian. Part of the experience of minor league baseball includes endless hours of free time between practices and games and during long, laborious road trips to small towns throughout the country.

My roommate and I used our free time to study, think, and especially debate. Each night guys would visit our room for spiritual discussions. I was a fairly new Christian who was regularly listening to and engaging in spiritual dialogue with atheists, agnostics, and a Mormon who had just finished a missionary assignment. Those nightly exchanges had a profound impact on my faith in a very positive way.

We hope it is refreshing for you to discover that asking questions for a better understanding of God's Word or *reasoning* is not wrong. Acts 17:16–34 describes the Apostle Paul reasoning in the synagogue with the Jews and God-fearing Greeks and in the marketplace with the philosophers. The Bible never asks you to shut off your brain. Unfortunately, some are still propagating the lie that you cannot ask hard questions and be a follower of Christ.

How did the Apostle Paul reason with the people from Athens?

What was the result of Paul's reasoning with the philosophers at the Areopagus?

Don't miss Acts 17:34, "Some of the people became followers of Paul and believed. Among them was Dionysius, a member of the Areopagus, also a woman named Damaris, and a number of others."

Paul's reasoning enabled some to come to faith. Here is what you need to know if you happen to encounter a person who has lots of questions like me:

+ Love the person. Don't reject him and attack him because he has questions. Love and acceptance are more powerful than an argument.

+ Acknowledge good questions.

+ Do not be offended that someone asks a question about a sacred issue. It is not wrong to ask questions about God.

+ You do not need to have all the answers. It is much better to say you do not know than to make up an answer. Detailed people notice small inconsistencies, and they enjoy pointing them out.

+ Tell the person, "I don't know the answer to that question" when you do not have an answer. Tell him you will try to find an answer for his question and then do it. It is loving to try to help someone find an answer to his question. While there may not be a definitive answer for every tough question, there are usually plausible ones. Some of the authors who wrestle with hard questions are: Lee Strobel, Josh McDowell, C. S. Lewis, and Ravi Zacharias. You could also ask your spiritual coach or your pastor for help as well.

+ You do not need to have a faith crisis because someone else has a difficult question. Stay close to Jesus. Let others' questions be their questions and yours be yours.

→ Pray for your friend. God can move a person from non-believing to believing. He often uses circumstances that have nothing to do with an argument to help a person get unstuck.

Do not shy away from those with difficult questions and do not be threatened by them. They are probably seeking real answers, and they certainly need the friendship that the body of Christ offers. Pray specifically for your friends. Ask God for wisdom to know how to love each one of them, especially those who need God to make sense. It might take awhile but if you love them and include them, some will come to Christ.

Prayer:
Praise God for forgiving you and for welcoming you into his family. Tell the Lord about your friends who need him. Ask God how you can serve them and love them.

ATTRIBUTE FOUR
DECISIONS

ATTRIBUTE FIVE

• • •

LEARN TO LOVE

ATTRIBUTE FIVE
INTRODUCTION
LEARN TO LOVE

DO YOU HAVE A FRIEND who HAS THAT WONDERFUL quality that the more you know them, the more you like them? You might not have recognized it at first, but the longer you hang out with the person, the more you appreciate them. Jesus is like that. The more you get to know him, the more you will love him, appreciate him, and want to be like him. That's partly why we spent two lessons encouraging you to get to know him. The foundation of everything else we are going to learn together flows out of your relationship with him. In one sense you never grow beyond that. It is always about remaining in him and enjoying your loving relationship with Jesus.

Because of what he gives to you, you realize you want to be able to give to him more of yourself out of gratitude. And, frankly, since life is so much better doing it his way, you don't want to hold anything back from him.

In the Overview of this book, where Attribute Two—Learn to Listen is summarized, we saw how being with Jesus leads us to people who need healing. Jesus healed and continues to heal people not only of spiritual pain but also of physical and emotional pain as well.

I (Daniel) was raised in a Christian home but we certainly had our problems. My mother struggled with bipolar disorder (manic-depression), but my parents both loved God and loved people. That's a pretty good start. At one point in my life, I thought we (my family and our particular brand of Christianity) had the corner on the truth market.

You can imagine how surprised I was to discover that some things I believed about God and the world were not true. It would take too long to explain where it came from, but I believed that my worth in life and with God was dependent on being perfect. I worked really hard to be perfect, but I just couldn't do it. So I always felt defeated and unloved. I also believed that I needed people's approval in order for me to feel good about myself. Perfectionism and approval addiction held me in bondage for years. I needed healing.

A friend of mine, who happened to be a counselor, told me about a book that changed my life, *The Search for Significance* by Robert McGee.[1] This book is about God, what he is like, and how he thinks about us. Although I had heard all my life that God was loving and accepting, somehow it didn't sink into my soul. So I continued to try to convince God to love me by attempting to be perfect or by my performance. I worked harder and harder but I couldn't earn God's love. When I discovered that I could not do anything to make God love me more or love me less, it changed my life. I remember sitting in seminary when that thought hit me. Later when I read McGee's book, I was able to apply this to my life. *The Search for Significance* helped me identify some lies that I believed about myself and God. You can be a follower of Jesus and still believe things that are not true. If you act on those lies, it will mess you up. The powerful truth I discovered was that because of Jesus' life, death, and resurrection, I am deeply loved, completely forgiven, fully pleasing, totally accepted by God, and absolutely complete in Christ. I am secure and significant in Christ.[2] I want you to be able to learn this at the beginning of your walk with God so you can enjoy, know, and love God for the rest of your life.

Jesus said, "The thief comes only to steal and kill and destroy; I have come that they may have life, and have it to the full" (John 10:10). The goal for this session is to help you understand the truth about who Jesus says you are so you can enjoy the full life he has planned for you. To do this, we need to do a little probing to see how deeply you believe certain common lies. You will take a brief self-scoring questionnaire each day to help you identify where you are with the lies. You will also discover the truth about those lies so you can walk in freedom from now on. Are you ready? I want to pray for you as you continue your journey.

Prayer:

Heavenly Father, I believe you are good. You have done so much for us in Jesus Christ. Help my friends discover the truth about who you are and who they are in you so they can walk in freedom before you the rest of their life. Amen.

ATTRIBUTE FIVE · STEP ONE
TRUST GOD

Scripture Memory (new):

[37] Jesus replied: "'Love the Lord your God with all your heart and with all your soul and with all your mind.' [38] This is the first and greatest commandment. [39] And the second is like it: 'Love your neighbor as yourself.'"
Matthew 22:37–39

Scripture Memory (review):　Matthew 4:19
　　　　Matthew 11:28–30　　Matthew 7:24–25
　　　　Matthew 7:7–8　　　Matthew 28:18–20

Take the Step 1–Trusting God Assessment on page 228.

Read: Luke 23:32–43

MANY PEOPLE STRUGGLE WITH BELIEVING God will forgive them. When we do not know we can be forgiven, there are only a few options for us. We might *work* to try to get God to like us and to forgive us (volunteer at church, help the poor, give money) in hopes that our good deeds will outweigh our bad deeds. We try to prove to God that we are worthy to be loved. But we always wonder if we did enough so we live under a cloud of fear. We might *ignore* the question of God's forgiveness, trying to not think about it. Since there is nothing we can do about it, why dwell on it? We might *minimize* our sin by saying "everyone does it" or "what I did wasn't as bad as..." We might get *angry at ourselves*. It is a terrible weight to remember what we have done. Some of us beat ourselves up emotionally or in other ways, thinking that if we hurt ourselves enough, maybe we will never do the bad deed again. We might even get *angry at God*. No one is perfect. "Since God is already upset with me for doing wrong, I might as well continue to do what pleases me." We might do even more things that we know displease God because we have given up trying to please him. We might *ask God to forgive* us as well.

What types of the responses do you see among the criminals crucified beside Jesus? ....

....

What was Jesus' response to the criminal who asked Jesus to remember him? ....

....

It is really important that you notice that Jesus accepted that criminal and that the criminal did nothing to deserve it. Jesus simply gave him the gift of forgiveness and relationship for eternity because he asked.

What is your normal response to dealing with memories of past failures? ....

....

My (Bryan's) natural inclination is to work. I tried various ways over the years to prove to others that I was worthy to be loved. This was especially true in high school when I was focused on becoming a good baseball player. I had a real performance mentality toward acceptance and approval. I really felt the better I performed the more I would be valued. While I did achieve some success, the feelings of happiness and self-worth were only temporary. I was coming to realize success in any area didn't necessarily lead to feeling significant. I often thought, "There must be more to life than this." Have you ever felt that way? If so, what did you do to try to find meaning in life?

One of the problems with thinking this way is that we think our value is established by what we do rather than what Christ has done for us. When we do this, we live our lives based on a lie, that our worth is dependent on us and not God.

Read Romans 5:6–11

Jesus already paid the price for your sin. There is nothing you can do to make God love you more or love you less. No matter how hard you work or how perfectly or imperfectly you serve him, he will not love you any more or any less than he does right now. What are your initial reactions to that statement?

How will knowing this truth affect the way you respond to God?

Prayer:

Thank you, Jesus, for dying on the cross for my sin. It amazes me that you would do that for me. Thank you for making me right before God and for giving me peace and your favor. I am truly grateful. Forgive me for trying to find my worth in something other than you. (You may want to confess some of these things right now if they come to your mind.) I choose to find my worth only in you from this day forward. I rest in you. Amen.

ATTRIBUTE FIVE · STEP TWO
SEEK GOD'S APPROVAL

Scripture Memory:

³⁷ Jesus replied: "'Love ____ ____ ____ ____ with all ____ heart and with ____ your soul and ____ all your ____.' ³⁸ This is the first and _____ commandment. ³⁹ And the second is ____ it: 'Love your _____ as yourself.'" _____ 22:37–39

³⁷ Jesus replied: "'Love the Lord your God with all your heart and with all your soul and with all your mind.' ³⁸ This is the first and greatest commandment. ³⁹ And the second is like it: 'Love your neighbor as yourself.'"
Matthew 22:37–39

Take the Step 2–Seeking God Assessment on page 230.

Read: Matthew 9:9–13; Colossians 1:21–22

ANGER, AVOIDANCE, AND APPROVAL are three powerful ingredients that affect every relationship we experience in life. Many books have been written about the negative impact that these emotions can have when they are out of control. The decision to follow Jesus brings the presence of the Holy Spirit into our lives and then he helps us to experience God's love which fills the voids in our lives that sin has opened. The way we have been raised, as well as many years of sinful choices, gives us a propensity to move toward anger, avoidance, and approval in an unhealthy manner. When you're not following Jesus as closely as you should, do you become a controller, an avoider, or a person constantly seeking approval?

I (Bryan) never really thought about this question until I took a graduate-level course on leadership. One of the texts we read was titled *Overcoming the Dark Side of Leadership: The Paradox of Personal Dysfunction* by Gary L. McIntosh and Samuel D. Rima.[1] The book points out that the same traits that drive us to succeed have the potential of bringing out a dark side of our leadership. I am a recovering pleaser. I don't understand all the reasons for that, but I know for many years I believed my self-worth was based on what others thought of me or my performance. If I was liked or esteemed, I felt good. When someone disapproved of me, I felt bad. It created the following cycle in my life: work hard, achieve, receive praise, feel unfulfilled, decide I needed to work harder, repeat. I repeated that cycle many times.

I applied the same approval pattern to my relationships with others and with God until I became a Christian, and then I began to realize that my efforts and achievements would never fulfill me. I had to allow the Scriptures to transform my thinking about seeking the approval of others. I wish I could say by the time I entered full-time ministry I was completely delivered from that cycle, but that wasn't true. I remember praying to the Lord on one occasion, which actually thinking about it now was more complaining than praying. I remember asking God to let me just be a normal Christian because I was feeling the stress and pressure of life and full-time ministry. I wanted God to pat my head and tell me I would be fine, but he showed me something different. He revealed to me Jeremiah 31:14, "'I will satisfy the priests with abundance, and my people will be filled with my bounty,' declares the LORD." It was a powerful revelation in my life. If I would be satisfied with God's abundance, then the people I was ministering to would be filled with God's goodness rather than mine. It's important to see how God sees us, and that God's approval, and unfailing love is what will really satisfy and break the cycles of anger, avoidance, or approval.

You can see how Jesus thinks about people from the story you read today from Matthew 9:9–13. Matthew was a tax collector. To get that job, he had to collaborate with the hated Roman government so he could legally steal money from his friends and family. The tax amount was never published, so he could name his own price and pocket the excess after he gave the unpublished but required amount to Rome. People hated the tax collectors because they knew this was happening. But Jesus looked past all of that and he saw a person whom he loved. While Matthew was still in his sin, Jesus loved him and invited him to follow. Jesus also loved Matthew's friends who were equally in need. That's what Jesus is like. He has always been a friend of people like Matthew, his friends, and anyone else who knows they need forgiveness. He is a friend of sinners like me and you.

When you don't know that, it can really mess you up. If you want God's approval, you may try to work really hard. I was surprised and relieved to discover this way of thinking was directly related to a false belief: "I must be approved by certain others to feel good about myself."

According to Colossians 1:22, what has Jesus done for us? ....

....

The word "reconcile" means "to make friendly again, to settle a quarrel." Notice that "reconciled" is a past tense verb. According to this passage, what event reconciled you to God and what was the result? ....

....

It would be hard to describe how freeing it has been to discover that I do not have to work anymore to please God. Many people, Christians included, feel unloved, unaccepted, and lonely because they believe the lie that God's love and approval has to do with their behavior. Just so I make sure you get it, whose behavior makes you approved by God?

You can start your walk with Jesus by knowing the truth that God loves and approves of you because of what Jesus did for you. Because of what Jesus did for you, you are holy, without blemish, and free from accusation. Take a deep breath right now and think about and enjoy God's approval.

Write the following sentence on an index card and repeat it throughout the day: "I am deeply loved, completely forgiven, fully pleasing, totally accepted by God."

How will knowing this truth affect your life?

Prayer:

Thank you, Heavenly Father, for accepting what Christ did for me on the cross. I am grateful for your acceptance and approval because of that. I turn away from trying to perform to find my value. Help me to accept myself the way you accept me. Help me to focus only on resting in you and enjoying your approval. Help me to accept those around me the way you accept them, to encourage them to be the individuals you have made them to be. I rest in your approval today. Amen.

ATTRIBUTE FIVE · STEP THREE
ENJOY GOD'S ACCEPTANCE

Scripture Memory:

³⁷ _____ replied: "'Love _____ _____ _____ _____ with all _____ _____ and with _____ _____ _____ and _____ _____ your _____.' ³⁸ This is the _____ and _____ _____ _____. ³⁹ And the second is _____ it: 'Love your _____ as _____.'"
Matthew _____:37–39

---

³⁷ Jesus replied: "'Love the Lord your God with all your heart and with all your soul and with all your mind.' ³⁸ This is the first and greatest commandment. ³⁹ And the second is like it: 'Love your neighbor as yourself.'"
Matthew 22:37–39

Take the Step 3–Enjoying God's Acceptance Assessment on page 232.

Read: Luke 7:36–50

THE STORY IN LUKE 7:36–50 MOVES ME every time I read it. Although the woman was obviously a "sinner," Jesus received her act of love without embarrassment, and he gave her salvation and peace. He accepted her, something the Pharisee, at whose home they were eating, could not do. In this story, Jesus makes the point that those who have been forgiven much, love much.

I have met many people who believe those who fail are unworthy of love and deserve to be punished. They might not say it that bluntly, but their belief shows up in a variety of actions. They feel justified in condemning others who fail, including themselves. They may call others or themselves names, "I am so stupid for..." or, "He's such a loser..." They might make jokes or cutting remarks about others' failures or they make self-deprecating statements about their own short-comings. They might say harsh words (verbally abuse) or they physically abuse themselves or others. But the bottom line is that someone around them has to pay when failure occurs. The thought behind that belief is this, "Those who fail are unworthy of love and deserve to be punished."[1]

That is also why it is hard to deal with ourselves when we fail. None of us is without sin. The truth is that none of us really want justice. I have heard it said, "We want justice for others but grace for ourselves." Romans 3:23 states, "All have sinned and fall short of the glory of God." Some try to convince themselves they do not sin but 1 John 1:8 tells us, "If we claim to be without sin, we deceive ourselves and the truth is not in us." Romans 6:23 tells us the payment for that sin, "For the wages of sin is death." Since we all have sinned and we all deserve death, we all have a problem. If we get justice, we will be separated from God forever. If we don't get justice then God would be a liar. So we are stuck. Furthermore, Hebrews 9:22 states, "Without the shedding of blood there is no forgiveness." Someone has to die so we do not have to be separated from our Creator. 1 John 4:10 tells us how Jesus Christ provides the solution for our dilemma.

Summarize 1 John 4:10 in your own words.

God sent his Son Jesus to atone for our sins. "Atone" means "to make amends." God sent Jesus to make amends for our sins so we don't receive what we deserve—death and separation from God. It is sobering but it's awesome! God loves you and wants you to have a relationship with him so much that he even paid the price for everything you have done that was wrong: past, present, and future.

That sets up a new life paradigm for us. According to 1 John 4:11, what impact will God's atonement have on your relationships?

Based on this passage, how might God's love affect the way you look at yourself when you fail?

How might it affect the way you treat others when they fail?

Have you ever seen this modeled? If so, describe what that person was like.

I (Daniel) learned from Robert McGee in the book *The Search for Significance* that the way out of the failure/punishment pattern is to accept and experience God's love. He suggests meditating many times each day on this thought, "I am deeply loved, completely forgiven, fully pleasing, totally accepted by God, and complete in Christ."[2]

Take the next few minutes right now and think about that statement. Say each phrase slowly and let the truth of God's Word seep into your spirit. The internal change you experience because of his love could impact every day of the rest of your life.

***Prayer*:**

Thank you, Heavenly Father, for sending Jesus to pay for my sins completely. I am truly grateful that you have accepted me and that I am complete in Christ. Thank you for welcoming me and inviting me to talk with you right now, freely and openly. That means so much to me. Teach me how to extend the same love and acceptance to others that you freely give to me. Amen.

ATTRIBUTE FIVE · STEP FOUR
PARTNER WITH GOD TO CHANGE YOU

Scripture Memory:

³⁷ Jesus_____: "'Love ___ ___ ___ ___ with ___
___and with ___ ___ ___ and _____ ___your ___.'
³⁸ ___ is the ___ and _____ _____ . ³⁹ And the
___ is ___it: '___ your _____ as _____.'"
Matthew 22:___ – ___

---

³⁷ *Jesus replied: "'Love the Lord your God with all your heart and with all your soul and with all your mind.'* ³⁸ *This is the first and greatest commandment.* ³⁹ *And the second is like it: 'Love your neighbor as yourself.'"*
Matthew 22:37–39

Take the Step 4–Partnering with God to Change You Assessment on page 234.

Read: John 7:53–8:11; Titus 3:3–7

HAVE YOU EVER THOUGHT, "I AM WHAT I AM. I cannot change"? Or, "That's the way I've always been, and that's the way I'll always be"? Have you ever turned down an offer to do something you really wanted because you did not want to embarrass yourself or others if you failed? If so, your sense of who you are and your opinion of your past failures are keeping you from enjoying the life God has for you. Both of the passages you read today provide hope for you. With

God's help, you can change.

To move out of this kind of thinking and into the new life God has for you, you need a perspective that is based on God's unconditional love and acceptance. Your past failures are a reality, but so is God's unconditional love. To move out of feeling shameful about yourself, you will need to value God's view of you more than your view of your past failures.

You know you are struggling with this kind of thinking if you are not pursuing something you really want or need because you are afraid of rejection or failure. The threat of rejection may cause you to withdraw from people and social situations, especially if you are afraid you just won't measure up.

Those who struggle with this way of thinking often struggle with a sense of inferiority, habitually destructive behavior, self-pity, passivity, isolation and withdrawal, loss of creativity, codependent relationships, and despising their appearance.[1]

God has a much better way. It is called "regeneration." The moment you began to trust Christ, he made you a new person. 2 Corinthians 5:17 says, "Therefore, if anyone is in Christ, the new creation has come; the old has gone, the new is here!" Everything you and I have ever done was completely forgiven when we trusted Christ. Everything! Because you are no longer held captive by your past and because you are a new person in Christ, you can change. Say out loud, "Because I'm a new person in Christ, I can change. I no longer need to experience the pain of shame."

What did Jesus say to the woman caught in adultery after everyone left? ....

....

Notice that while others would condemn her to die, Jesus defended her right to live and then gave her hope that she could start a new life. Jesus does that for you as well.

Change may not be easy but it will be worth it. In order to change you need to internalize what God's Word says about you. Summarize Titus 3:3 in your own words.

According to Titus 3:4–5, what prompted God to save you and how did he do it?

It is really important that you realize and accept that Jesus saved you not because of righteous things you have done but because of his mercy. Notice that "he saved us" is in the past tense. Jesus did the work to save all of us "by the washing of rebirth and renewal by the Holy Spirit." He washed you and renewed you. You may not always feel like a new person but God's Word tells you the truth about yourself. He gave renewal to you as a gift. That was God's part.

God's kindness makes you want to serve him. God gives you a gift (grace) and your response is gratitude. According to Romans 12:1–2, what is your part in the renewal process?

What do these verses say is your response to God's mercy?

What needs to happen so you no longer conform to the pattern of this world?

What will happen when you do this?

Why not talk to God right now about your decision to present your body to him. He sees your heart and he will help you change.

Prayer:

Dear Heavenly Father, I am amazed by your kindness and love for me. Thank you for saving me, not because of anything I did but because of your mercy. Thank you for washing my life and for renewing me by your Holy Spirit. I accept this as a gift from you. In view of your mercy, I present my body to you as a living sacrifice. Make me holy and pleasing to you. Renew my mind as well so I can think differently about my life. I want to change. Amen.

ATTRIBUTE FIVE · STEP FIVE
ENJOY GOD'S PEACE

Scripture Memory:

37 _____ : "" _____
_____ ,
38 _____ 39 ___
_____ : ' _____ "'
_____ : __ — __

> ³⁷ *Jesus replied: "'Love the Lord your God with all your heart and with all your soul and with all your mind.'³⁸ This is the first and greatest commandment. ³⁹ And the second is like it: 'Love your neighbor as yourself.'"*
> *Matthew 22:37–39*

Read: Philippians 4:4–7

A S YOU STUDY THIS ATTRIBUTE, you may be reframing what you believe about yourself and others by what God says about us. You have explored four lies that can keep you from the abundant life that God offers through Jesus. Today, you will learn how to be free from worry and anxiety. See if you can identify the four commands in Philippians 4:4–7.

This passage teaches us that God can help us learn how to be at peace in all circumstances. The four commands show us how: rejoice (v. 4), be gentle (v. 5), do not be anxious

(v. 6), present your requests to God (pray) (v. 6).

Let's be honest. We are not always happy. Painful and difficult things happen that make us sad, confused, or angry. What kinds of things are you going through right now that do not make you happy?

....

....

It is critically important that you understand the difference between being happy and rejoicing in the Lord. Happiness is based on experiencing pleasant circumstances and results, yet we all know that life's situations are not always pleasant. Joy, on the other hand, is the outcome of our relationship with Jesus rather than just emotion. You can rejoice in the Lord, however, all the time because he is in control of life's situations. The truth of Romans 8:28 helps me with this, "And we know that in all things God works for the good of those who love him, who have been called according to his purpose." No matter what comes your way, happy or sad, you can always trust God to work things out for the good if you love him. The question you need to ask yourself is, "Do I love God?" If you love him, you can depend on him always. Faithfulness is part of God's character. Your joy is not dependent on your circumstances. It depends on God's character and that never changes. That's why you can rejoice in the Lord always.

Second, when someone hurts you, don't you sometimes want to hurt them back? This passage teaches us that you can always be gentle to everyone. The Greek word for "gentle" means "to show forbearance toward someone." It is the quality shown by friends who know one another's idiosyncrasies and weaknesses but like each other anyway. Harshness, on the other hand, can be expected from an enemy. Don't confuse gentleness, however, with weakness. You can be gentle and still do the tough thing. It takes real strength to treat others gently, even when they deserve otherwise. This passage says you can be gentle to everyone because the Lord is near. In what situations or with whom do you struggle being gentle?

Third, this passage teaches us that we do not ever have to be anxious. Anxiety is worrying about things you cannot change. Jesus taught his followers that worrying is worthless. It doesn't change a thing. He said, "Can any one of you by worrying add a single hour to your life?" (Matthew 6:27). The assumed answer to that question of course is, "No." Corrie Ten Boom, a Holocaust survivor said, "Worry does not empty tomorrow of its sorrow, it empties today of its strength." If you put your life in God's hands, you can trust him to take care of you. Change what you have the power to change and leave the rest with God.

What kinds of things are causing you anxiety right now?

Finally, the best way to handle anxious thoughts is to present them to God. That's another way of saying "pray." Talk to God about the things that are on your mind. You can tell him exactly what you are thinking and how you feel. I do a lot of this in my confidential journal. Whether you do it in writing or out loud, just pour out your soul to God. Tell him how you feel and what you are thinking. He already knows, but it is emotionally healthy to get it out. God can handle your struggles. He is strong.

The result of rejoicing, being gentle, not being anxious, and presenting your requests to God will be peace, "The peace of God, which transcends all understanding, will guard your hearts and your minds in Christ Jesus." God's peace will guard your mind. You can be joyful, gentle, and free from anxiety at all times and in all circumstances. Let the truth of that start to sink into your mind right now.

Prayer:

Take some time right now to talk with God about whatever is on your mind.

ATTRIBUTE FIVE

DECISIONS

ATTRIBUTE SIX

• • •

LEARN TO PRAY

ATTRIBUTE SIX
INTRODUCTION
LEARN TO PRAY

PAUL TOLD THE FOLLOWERS IN PHILIPPI, "Don't worry about anything; instead, pray about everything" (Philippians 4:6a NLT). The power of prayer will positively impact relationships, circumstances, and lives. I (Bryan) always loved to listen to my wife pray. Her faithfulness made me a better husband, father, and Christian. I remember with fondness how Lynn prayed; she would talk to God like he was her best friend, and she knew that nothing was too big or too small for him. The relationship Lynn had with God through her prayer life during her time here on earth certainly prepared her to spend eternity with him in heaven! Lynn had a real relationship with God, one based on a close, intimate connection, the kind that we sometimes reserve only for our friends.

Great friends are a special gift. Friends are the ones you call first when the doctor gives you bad news or when you get a promotion. They tell you when you have food on your face and when they think you are out of line. They also celebrate with you when you have a significant milestone. You might not see them for years, but when you get together, it is like you have never been apart. Great friendship is amazing.

I (Daniel) had that kind of friendship with my sister, Maralyn. Although she was twelve when I was born, she and I developed a unique friendship. You would think the age difference and the difference in our gender wouldn't have allowed it but somehow none of that mattered. When I was growing up, she served as a surrogate mother for me since my true mother often could not be there for me because of her bipolar disorder. During the tough teen years, my father allowed me to call my sister when I needed, to talk through what was on my mind. What a gift that was in an era when we paid up to thirty cents a minute! Our phone conversations kept me alive during a very difficult time in life. Those conversations were like water to my soul.

You may have noticed I am writing about my sister in the past tense. On January 4, 2009, Maralyn passed away from ALS (amyotrophic lateral sclerosis, also known as Lou Gehrig's disease). I thought you might enjoy reading part of her last blog that was written just seventy-two hours before she died:

> Water is essential to life, and even though food will no longer propel down my throat, I'm still drinking. Amazingly, I don't feel hungry ... but I am thirsty, and I'm drinking as much as I possibly can. Without divine intervention, I will get to heaven some time within the month.
>
> These 18 months since my ALS diagnosis have been the worst and best of my life. Worst because of my deteriorating body ... best because of my relationship with Christ.
>
> And I'm beginning to see my friendship with Jesus like water when I'm thirsty ... so essential to life. He is the real "living water" referred to in John 4:1–26.
>
> I have many lovely friends, but I've never before known a Friend SO close. Every day we have smiled, laughed, and cried together. And he has comforted me. I've asked his opinion, and he has nodded one way or the other. His close friendship has given me many new perspectives on this earthly life that I had never considered before. He's been closer than my skin...
>
> The only thing that makes me sad is realizing that this intimate friendship with him has been available to me all throughout my life, and I never chose it until now. I missed it ... big-time! I guess I was always so busy with my lists, projects, plans and events that I was too occupied to be open to such an idea. Oh, I did my devotions, but so often because I knew I "should." That's a different thing. Now I long to be with him, to feel his hug, to hear his voice, to see his smile. It's so different.

Here's a piece of motherly advice: Don't wait until you have a terminal illness to seek a true friendship with Jesus. He's ready! It takes setting aside some less important things. It takes listening. It takes openness. But it's so worth it! I hope you become literally thirsty for Jesus.

Soon I'll be in heaven, and it will be great to see the scenery, gardens and mansions. It will be great to hear the singing and see what's on the banquet tables. BUT! I can tell you, the thing I'm most looking forward to is meeting my Best Friend face-to-face for the very first time. I'm trying to imagine the thrill...[1]

I don't know about you but reading that makes me want to get to know Jesus better. Let's talk with him now.

Prayer:

Jesus, we join your followers who once asked you, "Lord, teach us to pray." We ask that you will teach us like you taught them. We want to draw close to you and to hear your thoughts. We also want our lives to align with your plans for us. So teach us. Thank you for the invitation to follow you into a deeper walk with the Father. Amen.

ATTRIBUTE SIX · STEP ONE
DECIDE NOT TO PRAY BAD PRAYERS

Scripture Memory (new):

⁹ "This, then, is how you should pray: 'Our Father in heaven, hallowed be your name, ¹⁰ your kingdom come, your will be done on earth as it is in heaven. ¹¹ Give us today our daily bread. ¹² Forgive us our debts, as we also have forgiven our debtors. ¹³ And lead us not into temptation, but deliver us from the evil one.'" Matthew 6:9–13

Scripture Memory (review):   Matthew 4:19
Matthew 11:28–30   Matthew 7:24–25
Matthew 7:7–8   Matthew 28:18–20
Matthew 22:37–39

Read: Matthew 6:5–8

PRAYER IS SIMPLY TALKING WITH AND LISTENING TO GOD. Does it surprise you that Jesus teaches them how *not* to pray? In these verses, what does Jesus say not to do when you pray?

Jesus made it clear that prayer is not supposed to be something you do to display your spirituality. When you do that, prayer becomes about you. That is exactly what prayer is not. That's not to say you should never pray in public. It should just never be something you do to look holy. No one is holy except Jesus. When you talk with God in private, however, your Heavenly Father will reward you.

Jesus also taught in Matthew 6:7 not to "keep on babbling like pagans, for they think they will be heard because of their many words." Some people think they will get God's attention if they ask over and over, if they just bug him enough. Jesus was kind enough to tell us we cannot manipulate God to do anything just because we ask him a thousand times. God already knows our needs before we ask (Matthew 6:8).

I know I already talked about having a quiet time, but I want to keep it in front of you so it becomes a habit. Getting alone with God is something everyone can do. You may need to get up fifteen minutes earlier in the morning but you can do it. To pray like Jesus, you will need to find a time and a place that you will not be disturbed. For me it needs to be in the morning. I am not by nature a morning person but spending time with God is important enough to me that I try to do it first thing in the morning. I also find it helpful to go to a room away from my home office and the computer so I am not distracted. What time and place works best for you?

Prayer:
Take time right now to talk with God about your desire to continue to learn to pray.

ATTRIBUTE SIX · STEP TWO

LEARN THE DISCIPLES' PRAYER— PART I

Scripture Memory:

⁹ "This, then, is how you should ____: 'Our _____ in heaven, _____ be your ____, ¹⁰ your _____ come, your ____ be done on ____ as it is in _____. ¹¹ Give us today our____ ____. ¹² Forgive us ___ debts, as we also have _____ our debtors. ¹³ And lead us not ____ _____, but _____ us from the evil one.'" _____ 6:9–13

⁹ *"This, then, is how you should pray: 'Our Father in heaven, hallowed be your name, ¹⁰ your kingdom come, your will be done on earth as it is in heaven. ¹¹ Give us today our daily bread. ¹² Forgive us our debts, as we also have forgiven our debtors. ¹³ And lead us not into temptation, but deliver us from the evil one.'" Matthew 6:9–13*

Read: Matthew 6:9–13

AS A 51-YEAR-OLD MAN who spent most of my life doing things that would be considered active—playing baseball, playing racquetball, riding my motorcycle, running after my three boys—the last thing I (Bryan) ever thought I would need to do as an adult is to learn to walk again. But on June 7, 2015, when the motorcycle accident caused me to lose my left leg from above the knee on down, that is exactly the situation I found myself in.

The realization that I needed to re-learn a skill that I had taken for granted since I was a small child was a bit overwhelming at first. To think that my grandson, who was born a few months after the accident, would probably be able to walk better than me really was a humbling thought!

I've learned from my physical therapist that there is a lot that goes into our ability to take a step. As an amputee, my sensory system, which is the feedback we get when our feet hit the ground and is sensed in our skin, joint receptors, and muscles, is now different than when I was able to walk on two legs. People who are missing a toe, foot, or leg rely more heavily on their other leg. Therefore it has been much easier for me to walk at slow speeds because it is easier to control slower movement. As someone who always prided myself in getting where I wanted and needed to go quickly, this has been a very difficult "new normal" for me.

But a dear friend sent me an encouraging note after the accident. She closed that note with the Swahili phrase "haba na haba," which translated means "little by little." That phrase explains perfectly what the process to learn to walk again has been. It has been little by little. By setting attainable goals and working hard toward them, I found myself months, perhaps even years, ahead of my original prognosis!

It is still amazing to think that I needed to start at the very beginning again. Most of us can't relate to needing to learn how to walk again as an adult. But many of us have had the experience of needing to learn something new that seems overwhelming, difficult, and even unnatural.

Learning to pray is like learning to walk again. You may feel awkward and uneasy, but a little instruction, little by little, can go a long way.

In one sense, prayer is easy. It is simply talking to God about what's on your mind and then listening to whatever he says to you through his words (the Bible), through your thoughts, or through others.

The first followers of Jesus wanted to learn how to pray so they asked Jesus to teach them (Luke 11:1). We have already talked about the Lord's Prayer in the Overview of Attribute Six. In the next two days we are going to unpack that a little so you can learn how to pray with as little pain as possible. Jesus taught his followers six things about prayer. There are three Rs and three Fs. We'll talk about the three Rs today and the three Fs tomorrow.

Relationship—"Our Father in Heaven" teaches us that we are in a loving relationship with our Heavenly Father. Your Heavenly Father loves you so much. He longs for you to turn to him and to enjoy his presence. He welcomes you and enjoys being with you regardless of what you are going through, negative or positive. He cares about all your concerns. You may or may not have had a good father. But God will never leave you or forsake you. I know I already mentioned God's compassion in Attribute Three–Step 5, but I never get tired of hearing it: "The LORD is compassionate and gracious; slow to anger, abounding in love." Any other view of God needs to be set aside in view of an accurate one.

Take a minute or two right now and thank God for being your Heavenly Father. Tell him that you love him and that you are grateful that he is caring for you. Open your heart to him.

Respect—"Hallowed be your name" teaches us that God is completely pure (holy) and as such is worthy to receive our honor and respect. Something good happens when we start with honoring and respecting God. Don't start with talking about your needs in prayer. We will get to that later, but it should not be the first thing. Tell the Lord how much he means to you and honor him. You may want to kneel right now to show your respect to God. Some people will sing a song or two to God. There are a variety of worship styles. I like songs like "Here I am to Worship,"[1] "How Deep the

Father's Love for Us,"[2] "I Give You My Heart,"[3] "Indescribable,"[4] "More Than a Friend."[5] (You can purchase these from iTunes for about one dollar each.) Pour out your love and respect as you sing to God. Don't hold back here. He is worthy of all the honor and glory you and I can give him and more. When you meet with your coach, ask them if they have some favorite songs or other ways they respect and honor God.

Take time right now to tell the Lord you honor him and respect him. Acknowledge that he is completely pure and that he never has a bad thought or a bad idea. Honor him with your whole heart.

Reign—"Your kingdom come" teaches us to start with what God wants. You were not designed to "pull your own strings." When you pray "let your kingdom come," you are inviting God to be your leader and guide, to rule your life. You bow your life before him and you affirm that you belong to God, that you are committed to doing things his way. When you pray "let your kingdom come," you are inviting God to have complete control of your life.

Take time right now to ask God to rule in every area of your life. Talk with God about areas in your life over which you have difficulty giving up control: a job, a relationship, your future. You may find it helpful to write them down and then to share them with your coach.

ATTRIBUTE SIX · STEP THREE

LEARN THE DISCIPLES' PRAYER—
PART 2

Scripture Memory:

⁹ "This, _____, is _____ you should _____: ' _____ _____ in _____ , _____ be your _____ , ¹⁰ your _____ _____ , your _____ be _____ _____ _____ as it is in _____ . ¹¹ _____ _____ today our _____ _____ . ¹² _____ _____ debts, as we also have _____ our _____ . ¹³ _____ _____ _____ _____ _____ , but _____ us _____ the _____ one.'" Matthew _____:9–13

---

⁹ *"This, then, is how you should pray: 'Our Father in heaven, hallowed be your name, ¹⁰ your kingdom come, your will be done on earth as it is in heaven. ¹¹ Give us today our daily bread. ¹² Forgive us our debts, as we also have forgiven our debtors. ¹³ And lead us not into temptation, but deliver us from the evil one.'"*
Matthew 6:9–13

Read: Matthew 6:9–13

I N THE PREVIOUS STEP, WE TALKED ABOUT the three Rs of prayer. Can you remember what they are? ....

....

Take a few minutes now and pray the three Rs: Relationship, Respect, and Reign. Review yesterday if you need to.

In this step, we are going to talk about the three Fs.

Food—"Give us today our daily bread" teaches us that we can ask God to meet our basic needs. When our lives are lined up with his values, we can ask for fuel to do it. You may not be concerned today about whether or not you will have food. Most Americans have that covered pretty well… better than well. I (Bryan) enjoy food with all its smells and flavors. I also enjoy the preparation aspect of a meal. I love doing the food shopping for our family, going to the market and buying fresh items, and then coming home and actually doing the cooking. Sometimes I can easily forget that food is not just for enjoyment but for sustenance. If we don't keep a healthy balance between these two, it can adversely impact our health, focus, and self-esteem. When I pray for the Lord to give me my daily bread, I realize that means I need to eat within the range of my daily needs. We don't often think about prayer and food going together, other than a prayer of thanksgiving before everyone digs in. Within the Lord's Prayer, daily bread speaks not only of faith for daily provision, but also of the discipline to live with balance and moderation. This is an area where there is always room to grow as followers of Jesus. It is about having energy and strength to fulfill God's purpose for my life. When our hearts are aligned with God's heart, we can ask the Lord for food to help us. Take a moment right now and ask God to give you the food you need today to do his will for your life. How are you with food? Talk about this with your spiritual coach when you meet.

Forgiveness—"Forgive us our debts as we also have forgiven our debtors" teaches us that when we pray we remember we need forgiveness as much as everyone else. As I go before the Lord on a daily basis with my needs, prayers for others, and my personal sin as a follower of Jesus, it helps me dramatically forgive those who have sinned against me. Forgiveness is not forgetting the transgression or reestablishing the same trust level, but it is choosing not to make a person pay for what they did. Forgiveness refreshes our heart and spirit and brings us closer to Jesus. What helps me more than anything is realizing that I need forgiveness for all my sin just as others do. God in his mercy paid the price for all my sin, and yours as well, through the death of Jesus Christ on the cross. I do not deserve his forgiveness, but he gives it to me if I will receive it. Complete forgiveness is available to all through Jesus. You cannot pay for your sins. Jesus already paid for them. Because he did that for you, you can forgive others. Tremendous freedom awaits you. You don't have to hate anymore.

Freedom—"And lead us not into temptation but deliver us from the evil one" teaches us that God can help you win over every temptation. Most Americans think freedom means being able to do what you want whenever you want. This is not freedom. Proverbs 14:12 states, "There is a way that appears to be right, but in the end it leads to death." In other words, if you do what you think is right, eventually it will lead to destruction. Real freedom is being able to please God with the way you live, the reason for which you were created. With God's help we can be delivered from the things that are destroying us. That's why we need to ask for freedom from temptation and deliverance from the evil one. We need God's help to go in the right direction and to do the right things. If you ask God, he will help you with this.

Let the Lord's Prayer guide you as you talk with God now.

Prayer:

(**Relationship**) Thank you, Heavenly Father, for inviting me to be your child. It is wonderful to know you welcome me and care for me.

(**Respect**) Truly you are pure and worthy of all praise and honor. There is no one like you. You are amazing. I worship you with my whole being.

(**Reign**) I invite you to rule in my life today. Have

your way in me. Mold me and shape me in a way that brings honor to you. I invite you to have complete control of my life. Have your way in my home. Help me to love those around me like you want them to be loved.

(*Food*) Thank you for providing for my physical needs today, for food, shelter, and clothing. I have everything I need because you provide it. Help me to use every ounce of energy and all my resources for your purposes today.

(*Forgiveness*) Thank you for forgiving all my sins. (Admit to God any specific things you have done recently that you know are wrong.) I accept your complete forgiveness for my sins because of what Jesus did on the cross. Thank you. I forgive (name the person[s] you need to forgive) for (describe to God what the person did that hurt you). Because you forgive me, I can forgive them.

(*Freedom*) Guide me down the right path today. Help me to stay away from things that are destructive. Deliver me from (name the specific thing that you need freedom from). Thank you for the freedom I have because of the finished work of Jesus Christ. I am a new person today because of what you have done for me. I ask this in Jesus' name, amen.

ATTRIBUTE SIX · STEP FOUR
LEARN TO PRAY THROUGH PAIN

Scripture Memory:

⁹ "This, _____ , is _____ _____ _____ _____ : ' _____ _____ in
_____ , _____ _____ _____ _____ , ¹⁰ your _____ _____ ,
your _____ be _____ _____ as _ _ _ _ _ _ . ¹¹ _____ _ _
_____ our_____ _____ . ¹² _____ _ _ _ _____ , as we also have
_____ our _____ . ¹³ And _____ _ _ _____ _____ ,
but _____ us _____ the _____ one.'" Matthew 6: _ – _

⁹ *"This, then, is how you should pray: 'Our Father in heaven,*
hallowed be your name, ¹⁰ your kingdom come, your will be done
on earth as it is in heaven. ¹¹ Give us today our daily bread. ¹²
Forgive us our debts, as we also have forgiven our debtors. ¹³ And
lead us not into temptation, but deliver us from the evil one.'"
Matthew 6:9–13

Read: Matthew 6:14–15

OW DO YOU FORGIVE SOMEONE who has caused you so much pain? How do you look that person in the eye and tell them, with confidence and sincerely, that you truly forgive them? The motorcycle accident that took my wife of twenty-eight years and my left leg could have been avoided. Although the man who hit us head-on certainly had no intention to cause us harm, the choices he made will forever change my life, as well as the life of my family, our church, and our community. Choosing to drive with a blood alcohol level four times over the legal limit is a poor decision and an avoidable one. However, when I came face to face with the man responsible for my wife's death and the loss of my leg, I told him that, although he caused me pain that is almost indescribable, I completely and totally forgave him. Probably the one question I get the most from people is how I was able to forgive the man that took so much from me. My answer is always a simple one. I forgive because Christ forgave me. All of us have fallen short. Each of us needs forgiveness and if we have received that forgiveness, Jesus is calling us to extend that same forgiveness to others. That doesn't mean we forget what wrong has been done to us. I will never forget the pain and sorrow that young man caused me, but I won't live in the bitterness and anger that unforgivingness can cause.

Not forgiving can be like a cancer. If you are facing the inability to forgive someone for a past wrong, I encourage you to ask God to show you how to be free from the resentment that can build up when we live in a state of unforgivingness. Let the Lord teach you to forgive through a process. Consider making a list of the people who hurt you and the incidents in which you were hurt. It may take you quite a while to forgive everyone on your list, but once you do, you will feel like a new person. Only the grace of God will allow you to do this.

Write down the people or incidents you know you need to forgive. Don't wait. Do it now. You will probably add to your list as you remember things later. ....

....

....

....

Take one incident at a time to pray through this process:

1. *Pour out your soul to God* (Psalms 13, 51:17). Tell God about the specific event that caused you pain. Pour it

out. Tell him what happened and how you felt about it. Tell God about it until you know you have said everything that needs to be said. Don't censor yourself. God can take it. It might surprise you to find out there is a specific kind of psalm that is designed to help you pour out your heart to God when you are in pain. It is a called a "lament" psalm. There are more laments than any other type of psalm.[2] This ought to encourage you to be open with God about your pain. Tell him or write out what you think about what happened to you. (I find writing is more helpful to me. I can look at it and see it when I am done.) Tell God exactly how you feel. You can tell God your thoughts, pain, and concerns without worrying that he will be offended or shocked. It is healthy for you emotionally and spiritually to pour out your soul to God.

2. *Let God comfort you* (2 Corinthians 1:3–4). After you have poured out your heart, invite God into the painful memory. Ask God what he thinks about your painful situation. Listen to your thoughts and impressions at that point. He may remind you of a passage of Scripture. He may give you a new thought. He may give you a comforting picture. It is always different for me. Nothing can separate you from the love of God (Romans 8:39).

3. *Confess your sin* (1 John 1:9). What happened to you may have been sad or terrible, something that was not your fault. However, we all need to take responsibility for what we did afterwards. I hated people and tried to work harder to convince myself that I was worthy to be loved. That was against God's plan for my life. It was sin. You need to confess whatever you did as a result of your situation that was against God's principles. Confession is just agreeing with God that something you did was not right.

4. *Ask God to restore your soul* (Psalm 23:3; 2 Corinthians 5:17). 2 Corinthians 5:17 says, "Therefore, if anyone is in

Christ, the new creation has come; the old has gone, the new is here!" Rest for a few minutes in God's presence, knowing that you are restored to relationship with God.

5. *Identify the lie* (2 Corinthians 10:4–5; John 8:32). Behind every sinful act is a lie, something you believe about yourself, God, or another that is not true. As you think about the painful incident, what are your thoughts? You may want to write them down. What you told yourself as a result of the painful incident may hurt more than the incident itself. If you can identify the lie, you can replace it with the truth. You may need help from your spiritual coach, a pastor, or a counselor to identify the lie, but it is worth exposing it because the truth will set you free. I will give you an example. When my birth came up in conversation with my parents, I always heard that I was "a surprise." When I asked what that meant, my parents would always make a joke about it. In essence they would say they were not trying to have a child, but they were glad God gave me to them. As an adult, I know their preferred method of birth control did not work. As a child I heard, "I was a mistake. My parents did not really want me." There were circumstances that convinced me this lie was true. This lie became the backdrop and primary theme of my life until God helped me expose it as a lie. It would take too long to explore the ramifications of believing that lie, but I had to identify it so I could be set free by the truth.

6. *Replace the lie with truth* (Psalm 1; Philippians 4:4–9). You may need help to identify the truth about your situation. Talk this through with your spiritual coach. If he or she doesn't know, both of you can ask your small group leader or your pastor. If they can't figure it out, you may want to go to a good Christian counselor. There are several passages of Scripture that helped me replace my lie with the truth. Psalm 139:13–16 was powerful for me:

For you created my inmost being; you knit me together in my mother's womb. I praise you because I am fearfully and wonderfully made; your works are wonderful, I know that full well. My frame was not hidden from you when I was made in the secret place. When I was woven together in the depths of the earth. Your eyes saw my unformed body; all the days ordained for me were written in your book before one of them came to be.

According to God's Word, I was not a mistake. God thought about every day of my life before I was born. God decided that I would be born and he has a plan for my life. When I start to feel insecure or insignificant, I can tell myself the truth. God loves me. I'm here for a purpose. He knows everything about me and he has my life in his hands. I am secure in him. That truth changed my life.

Prayer:

Do you have some people or situations that you need to pray through? Your caring Heavenly Father can set you free through the process you have learned today. He used it to change my life. It may take months for you to get through your list but when you are done you will feel like a new person. And you will never want to go back to the old way. When you come to Jesus, you find rest for your soul. Why not take one incident or a person on your list and walk through the process right now. Freedom awaits you.

ATTRIBUTE SIX · STEP FIVE
LEARN TO DO SPIRITUAL WARFARE

Scripture Memory:

9 " ___ , ___ , ___ ___ ___ ___ ___ : '
___ , ___ ___ ___ ___ , 10 ___ ___ ___ , ___ ___ ___
___ ___ ___ ___ ___ 11 ___ ___
___ ___ ___ ___ . 12
___ ___ ___ ___ ___ , ___ ___
___ ___ ___ ___ . 13
___ ___ ___ ___ ___ ___ ,'" ___ ___ : ___ ___

9 *"This, then, is how you should pray: 'Our Father in heaven,
hallowed be your name,* 10 *your kingdom come, your will be done
on earth as it is in heaven.* 11 *Give us today our daily bread.* 12
Forgive us our debts, as we also have forgiven our debtors. 13 *And
lead us not into temptation, but deliver us from the evil one.'"*
Matthew 6:9–13

Read: Ephesians 6:10–20

THE BIBLE TEACHES THERE IS MORE TO THIS WORLD
than what you see. There is a real devil. There are rulers,
authorities, and dark powers in this world and spiritual forces
of evil in the heavenly realms (Ephesians 6:12). I wish it
wasn't so but it is. Their sole purpose is to resist the work of
God and to destroy your life. The evil one and his forces fight
dirty. Rarely do they attack head on. When you are tired,
hungry, or lonely, they move in to try to mess up your life.
Ephesians 6:10–20 shows you how to fight and win against
these destructive forces. There are eight commands in this

passage that show you how to win.

Read Ephesians 6:10 again. What are we commanded to do?

It is absolutely essential to know from where your strength comes. Notice it does not come from within you. It is the American way to try to be independent. Some of us will not ask for help unless we absolutely have to. If that is you, you are going to have to make a fundamental decision to find your strength in God and not in yourself. None of us are strong enough on our own to fight against the unseen forces of darkness. You will always win, however, if you depend on the strength of the Lord. No one is more powerful than God. It is the power of God that raised Christ from the dead. It is the power of God that brought the world into existence. It is the power of God that is changing your life. If you tap into his power, you cannot lose.

There are two questions you need to answer today. First, will you depend on the Lord for your strength or will you try to do it on your own? What is your decision?

What are some ways you depend on yourself rather than God?

Second, are you willing to learn how to fight in the spiritual realm? If you said "yes," the rest of today's guide will help you. Ephesians 6:11 is a summary statement for how to fight and win. First, you must "Put on the full armor of God." You cannot afford to only put on part of the armor of God. You need the full armor of God. You are vulnerable if part of you is exposed because you are missing proper armor.

Of all the players on a baseball field, the catcher wears more equipment than any of the other players. During every level of my baseball career from little league to the major leagues, I (Bryan) had to endure the routine of putting on the tools of the trade: a catcher's mitt, a helmet, mask, chest protector and shin guards. Each serves a very specific purpose for protection. Although the equipment was cumbersome and hot, a foul ball hit directly into my face mask always reminded me of the importance of its protection. I can't imagine getting behind the plate with only my glove. How many followers of Jesus walk onto the battlefield of life without using the equipment God provides?

You can be fully protected in spiritual battles. Notice that the word "stand" repeats in Ephesians 6:11, 13 (two times), 14. You can take your stand, resist the attacks of the evil one and not be shaken when you do spiritual warfare, if you put on the full armor of God. You need it all.

Armor Piece #1—The Helmet of Salvation. Accepting the finished work of Christ for you on the cross protects you from fatal head wounds. Take a moment to thank God that he saved you by dying on the cross for your sins. Don't try to work for it, just accept it and thank God now.

Armor Piece #2—The Sword of the Spirit which is the Word of God. The only offensive weapon you have is the Scriptures. Over the next months and years, as you immerse yourself in the Scriptures, you will discover how powerful the Word of God is.

Armor Piece #3—The Belt of Truth. When you know the truth found in the Scriptures, you are no longer vulnerable to the lies of Satan. One of the best questions you can ask yourself when you are tempted is, "What lie am I believing?" When you discover the lie and replace it with the truth expressed in Scripture, you win a battle. I find it fascinating that truth is linked to the middle part of our bodies, the sexual part of our bodies. The truth will affect every area of our lives, especially our sexual behaviors.

Armor Piece #4—The Breastplate of Righteousness. Righteousness is a gift from God that comes by faith in

Jesus Christ and it will guard your heart. 2 Corinthians 5:21 states, "God made him who had no sin to be sin for us, so that in him we might become the righteousness of God." Romans 3:22 states, "This righteousness is given through faith in Jesus Christ to all who believe." When you trust God to give you righteousness through Jesus, it keeps you from doing things to prove you are righteous. In spiritual warfare, the evil one might bring up your past and tell you how bad or unworthy you are. That is when you remind your enemy and yourself that you are righteous, not because of anything you have done but by faith in Jesus Christ. He makes you righteous. It is a gift, not something you earn.

Armor Piece #5—The Gospel of Peace. Romans 5:1 states, "Therefore, since we have been justified through faith, we have peace with God through our Lord Jesus Christ." You do not need to fear the attack of the evil one in the midst of spiritual warfare because God's peace is with you. Furthermore, there is a reason that peace is linked to your feet. God's peace has an active component to it. You must be prepared to bring God's peace to people who are lost.

Armor Piece #6—The Shield of Faith. A shield is a defensive weapon that keeps you safe from arrows that are sent your way. The evil one does not know your thoughts, but he does know how you acted in past situations. He is a student of your destruction. He will send fiery darts your way in the form of thoughts and opportunities to sin to see if you will accept them and then act on them: hateful thoughts, doubts, a burning desire to sin, a reminder of past hurts, et cetera. When those moments come, your faith in God will keep you from being destroyed. When you are tempted, by faith decide to act on what God's Word says and he will keep you safe.

Armor Piece #7—Praying in the Spirit. Notice how many times prayer is mentioned in Ephesians 6:18–20, "And *pray* in the Spirit on all occasions with all kinds of *prayers* and *requests*. With this in mind, be alert and always keep on *praying* for all the Lord's people. *Pray* also for me, that whenever I open my mouth, words may be given me so that I will fearlessly make known the mystery of the gospel, for which I am an ambassador in chains. *Pray* that I may declare it fearlessly, as I should" (emphasis mine). One of the powerful weapons you have in spiritual battle is prayer, talking with God. There are many different kinds of prayer available to you. Use them all. Praying in the Spirit is praying beyond your mind and words. Have you ever prayed for awhile and run out of words, but you feel like you are not done praying? That's the feeling I get right before I pray in tongues. There are many references in the Bible to people being empowered to pray in a heavenly language they never learned (Acts 2:4, 10:44–45, 19:6; 1 Corinthians 12:10, 12:30, 13:1, 14:1–25). The wonderful thing about praying in the Spirit is that the Spirit of God prays through you. Where your words are inadequate, the Holy Spirit can give you words in a heavenly language that adequately express to God what needs to be said. When we pray powerful prayers, powerful things happen. I believe the Bible teaches this experience is available to all believers for private prayer. Some people will use this in public prayer as well, but then there needs to be an interpretation. If you have never heard of this before, you may want to talk about this with your spiritual coach.

Prayer:

Heavenly Father, thank you for giving me the armor and the weapons I need to win in spiritual battle. Teach me how to use each piece of armor and the weapons of spiritual warfare. Enable me to win in battle against the spiritual forces of evil in the heavenly realms. Empower me to pray in the Spirit so I can pray more effectively. I need and want all you have for me. I want to be fully prepared for spiritual battle. Amen.

ATTRIBUTE SIX
DECISIONS

ATTRIBUTE SEVEN

· · ·

LEARN TO MANAGE

ATTRIBUTE SEVEN
INTRODUCTION
LEARN TO MANAGE

Read: Deuteronomy 6:4–5

"**K**OCH, DO YOU KNOW WHAT YOU REMIND ME OF?"

"What?" I replied.

"Kentucky Fried Chicken."

Sam was one of my coaches when I played for the White Sox, and this conversation occurred one day after a game where a pass ball through my legs almost cost us the win. I wondered why he compared me to KFC. Coming out of high school, I struggled a bit with minor league pitching. The strength of my game was defense. I had a strong arm, good hands behind the plate, and the ability to handle pitchers well. What Sam was saying was KFC does *one thing*, and they do it right. They make good chicken. He was reminding me to do the one thing I do, and to do it right. I needed to be a great defensive catcher or the reality of the situation was that I would come into the locker room one day, and my gear would be piled up with a plane ticket on top like a bow, and I would be headed back to Reading.

I (Daniel) went to school at a Christian liberal arts college where I was required to take a class called Basic Christianity. Since I was raised in a pastor's home and had spent so much time in church, I wondered what I could possibly learn in a Basic Christianity class. I wish it wasn't true, but I sat in the back of the class, fooled around, and talked with my friends. One day the teacher asked the class to identify the greatest commandment. Someone said, "Love the LORD your God will all your heart and with all your soul and with all your strength." The professor asked what that meant. We tried to define it as putting God first in our heart. When we were talking about loving God with our minds, the professor asked what we would say about someone who is capable of earning an A in a class but because the student fools around, stays out late, doesn't prioritize studying, et cetera (the stuff I was doing), ends up getting a C. We said the student was being irresponsible and lazy. The professor said, "Do you know what the Bible calls that?" We didn't. He said, "If doing your best for God is worship, then not doing your best would be sin." Wow! I had never made the connection before.

There is a powerful spiritual truth in these stories. As Christians we have one thing to do, and that is to love Jesus. If we do that, everything else will fall into place. This realization can change your perspective and many of your future decisions. All of life will become an opportunity to worship God. I don't work *so* he will love me. I work *because* he loves me. I love him and want to honor him in everything. Loving God involves every area of your life: time, energy, money, influence. Everything. Furthermore, God expects a return on his investment in our lives. God put you and everyone else on the planet at such a time as this with a divine plan to use your specific gifts for the advancement of his kingdom. Wrapping your head around that will impact every decision you make for the rest of your life. Work on doing that one thing, and doing it right.

As you take each step, you will look at a different aspect of your life and how to worship God in that aspect of your life: mind, money, body, speech, time. One final suggestion and then we will pray: Remember to focus on loving God as you develop healthy habits. Don't get discouraged as you start to work in these areas. Almost everyone needs support and encouragement as we develop these venues for loving God. This step is just a start. I want to pray for you.

Prayer:

Heavenly Father, thank you so much for loving me and my friends. Your kindness to us is amazing. You have forgiven us of our sins, the things that separated us from you. We are truly grateful. You have given us a hope and a future when we had nothing. As my friends are looking at their resources and how they can love you in everything, I ask you to continue to assure them of your unending love. Encourage them and help them establish good habits as an expression of that love. Lord, you have given us so much. Help us to use it to bring honor to you. In your name we pray, amen.

ATTRIBUTE SEVEN · STEP ONE
MANAGE YOUR MIND

Scripture Memory (new):
"But seek first his kingdom and his righteousness, and all these things will be given to you as well." Matthew 6:33

Scripture Memory (review):   Matthew 4:19
     Matthew 11:28–30   Matthew 7:24–25
     Matthew 7:7–8   Matthew 28:18–20
     Matthew 22:37–39   Matthew 6:9–13

Read: Philippians 4:8

WE ALREADY TALKED ABOUT THE VERSES right before this verse, Philippians 4:4–7, on Attribute Five–Step 5: how God gives you peace of mind when you rejoice in him always, are gentle to everyone, choose not to be anxious about anything, and pray about everything.

What is the one command in Philippians 4:8?

You might be surprised to discover the Greek word for "think" does not simply mean to "think" by trying to exclude other thoughts. It means "to reckon, evaluate, to consider, ponder, let your mind dwell on."[1] What you think about, you will become. What you dwell on is vitally important to your walk with Christ. Put simply, the Apostle Paul is not teaching his readers through this passage to only think about Christian books, movies, and music. He is teaching them (and us) to filter what is around you from a Christian perspective. You do this by intentional thinking. 2 Corinthians 10:4–5 reads:

> The weapons we fight with are not the weapons of the world. On the contrary, they have divine power to demolish strongholds. We demolish arguments and every pretension that sets itself up against the knowledge of God, and we take captive every thought to make it obedient to Christ.

To take your thoughts captive you need to notice what you are thinking, and then ask yourself if that thought helps you become obedient to God and his plan for your life. If the thought does not, you must reject it and replace it with the truth as defined by Scripture.

I like Philippians 4:8–9 because it gives a summary about how a spiritually healthy mind thinks. There are things we need to think about. What are they?

Today in our culture "truth" is under attack from nearly every conceivable arena. What is it? How do you know what it is? Some would say it is subjective or relative. What's true for you might not be true for someone else. Jesus said, "I am the way and the truth and the life" (John 14:6). In other words, Jesus said truth is a Person. If you want to know what truth is, you cannot look within yourself. Proverbs 14:12 states, "There is a way that appears to be right, but in the end it leads to death." Similarly, Jeremiah 17:9 states, "The heart is deceitful above all things and beyond cure. Who can understand it?" Jesus also said in John 17:17, "Sanctify them (the disciples) by the truth; your word is truth." Truth then is God's perspective as exemplified in Jesus and in God's Word.

People who work with money can identify counterfeit money quickly because they work with real money all day long. You will be able to identify what truth is by spending time with Jesus and in his Word.

Is there anything that God says about you or your life that you have a hard time believing?

You will want to share this with your spiritual coach so you can have his or her perspective.

What comes to mind when you think "noble?"

Noble means "honorable, worthy of respect, above reproach." If you are going to think about noble things, you may want to make some decisions about the kinds of movies or television shows you watch. I am not advocating hiding your head in the sand and avoiding what is unpleasant and displeasing. But if you know that the general tenor of a movie or show is not above reproach, you do not want to willfully expose yourself to it. There are better things about which to think. Do you need to make any adjustments regarding what you watch?

The Bible defines "right" as something that conforms to the laws of God and living in accordance to that. In other words, it is right if God says it is right. How might this understanding of "right" affect how you think about something?

Purity refers to moral purity. You are challenged to sort through the media and personal bombardment of sexual promiscuity in our culture and opt for the morally pure. Sexuality is not wrong. For example, it is morally pure to think about a scintillating memory of your spouse. Sexuality is pure within a monogamous marriage. It is not pure to lust after a two-dimensional image on a computer screen of someone who is not your spouse. Do you need to stop thinking some things which are not pure? If so, how will you do that?

What kinds of things do you need to start thinking about that are pure?

Lovely things are "cheerful, pleasing, and agreeable." They are beautiful. Music, nature, art, athletics can all be "lovely." When you filter life through what is lovely from God's perspective, you find beauty and then thank God for it. How might you dwell on what is truly lovely?

What kinds of things are admirable?

"Excellent" carries with it a sense of quality that includes virtue, morality, and integrity.

"Praiseworthy" means conduct worth talking about that is in keeping with God's moral character.

Read Philippians 4:9. What will happen if you think about these things and model your life after godly people?

There is nothing like having God's peace with you.

What adjustments do you need to make with your thought life?

What can you do to be more intentional about your thought life?

Do you need to stop a certain thought process that is not in keeping with God's will for your life? If so, what is it? How will you do it?

Prayer:

(Thank God for the freedom he offers you to learn how to think his thoughts. Tell God specifically how you intend to make changes in your thought life. Ask God to help you learn how to think in a way that honors him and brings you peace.)

Final thoughts:

I heard this summary about the impact of our thoughts:
Sow a thought, reap an action.
Sow an action, reap a habit.
Sow a habit, reap a character.
Sow a character, reap a destiny![2]

Proverbs 4:23 NCV, "Be careful what you think, because your thoughts run your life."

ATTRIBUTE SEVEN · STEP TWO
MANAGE YOUR MONEY

Scripture Memory:

"But seek _____ his kingdom and _____ righteousness, and _____ these things will be _____ to you as _____." _____ 6:33

"But seek first his kingdom and his righteousness, and all these things will be given to you as well." Matthew 6:33

Read: Matthew 6:19–33

URING MY (BRYAN'S) FORMATIVE YEARS no one in our home was really serving Jesus, yet my parents modeled many positive qualities for my sister and me. They taught us to be respectful of authority and to work hard for what we needed. We were taught that as members of the Koch household, we all had certain responsibilities to perform, and mine included keeping my room clean, mowing the grass, and taking out the garbage. My sister had her areas of responsibility as well. Like most families, mom and dad worked harder than anyone else.

There was one job in our home that was performed exclusively by my dad, and that particular responsibility was balancing the checkbook. I can still see him sitting at the kitchen table looking at each cancelled check and placing a mark in the ledger next to the entry. His commentary on each expenditure revealed his value of the transaction, and he was meticulous in matching the check with his record.

Although my dad did not maintain a written budget he kept us in good financial shape. My dad worked hard every day to provide for our family, and as my sister Marsha has often said, "Mom and Dad really positioned us for success."

The informal financial training I learned around the kitchen table taught me to live within my means and appreciate the principle of delayed gratification. One memory stands out above the rest in this regard. My dad always tried to buy the best when it was a necessity, but he didn't see everything as a necessity. Take for instance sneakers. Dad believed Chuck Taylors made by Converse were the best money could buy. He won a high school state championship in basketball wearing them and they were only twelve dollars a pair. Years later, Converse came out with a new design that I thought was the coolest sneaker I had ever seen. They were made with suede leather, sported the traditional Converse star, and came in some very cool colors; however, my dad's budget for sneakers was still only twelve dollars, and if I wanted to upgrade, I would have to wait and save. Although several of my friends had their suede Converse sneakers first, when I finally had the money to buy them, I doubt anyone appreciated the sneakers more than I did. I couldn't see it at the time but Jesus used experiences like that to begin to teach me how to manage the resources he would give me in the future.

I (Daniel) grew up in a lower-middle-class family. We always had food to eat, a place to sleep, and clothes to put on our bodies. Although my mom was a good cook, we did not eat the best food. Our homes were usually small. I often shared a bedroom with my brother and my closet usually had someone else's stuff in it. I often felt out of place and sometimes was made fun of at school because of my clothes. Even though we did not have the best clothing or athletic equipment, my brother and I were good athletes and that helped. But I was always aware that we were on the lower side of the economic scale. I also always knew that the reason for this was that my father was a minister. My parents never said or insinuated that we were deprived because they were ministers. In fact, they thought we were blessed. But the older I got, the more I vowed that when I grew up, I would not be poor. As I look back now, especially after traveling to difficult places in the world, I realize I had a pretty good life. At the time, however, I internalized that I was deprived. I compensated for these feelings by starting small businesses and dreaming about being rich. My thoughts were something like, "We live in America, the land of opportunity. I will get a great job, work hard, make lots of money, and enjoy the life that I deserve." I made a vow to myself to never be a minister because they don't make much money.

When I was twenty years old, Jesus put his finger on that part of my life, the desire for money and things. One night when I was having my quiet time with God, he challenged me to surrender to him my love for money. It was a great struggle. I had many questions and much anxiety about the future but I finally did it. I had only a little bit of cash at the time, but the Lord prompted me to give it all away. It was a summer between college years, and I was staying with my parents. I knew I would have a place to stay and food to eat, but it was a big deal for me to surrender that part of my life to God. However, it was one of the best decisions I have ever made. Seeing how God responded to me, and the joy I had from knowing I had surrendered that to God, far outweighed the financial ups and downs I have had since. God has always supplied my needs, and I have the great joy of knowing that he, rather than money, is at the center of my life.

Jesus addresses this area of your life in Matthew 6:19–33. We already discussed Jesus' warning against storing up for yourself treasures on earth.[1] Your heart will go where you put your treasure. Furthermore, Jesus tells us the truth that we cannot serve God and money (Matthew 6:24).

At this point in your life, would you say that you are serving money?

If so, what impact does it have on your life?

Would you like to make a change in this area of your life? Why or why not?

If you decided to make a change, what would that look like for you?

In Matthew 6:25–32, Jesus talks about why worrying is worthless. What are some reasons Jesus gives for why that is so?

In Matthew 6:33, what does Jesus tell you to do instead of worrying?

What decision(s) would you like to make based on the truths described in Matthew 6:19–33?

We could tell you many stories of God's provision but those are our stories. You need your own stories about what God has done because you surrendered your money to him. You and the Lord can write a new story together of God's faithfulness and miraculous provision. You will never know what that story would have been if you don't surrender. God is amazing. He does all things well. Trust him. Make the decision to follow him with your finances and don't look back. We have never regretted the decisions to surrender our finances to God. God has blessed us in so many ways because of that. We want that for you, and we know he does as well.

If you would like to know how to take practical steps with your finances, you can sign up for the next "Financial Peace University" seminar. You can also talk with your spiritual coach about this. He or she may have some suggestions for the next steps about how to put God first in your finances.

> ### *Prayer:*
> Heavenly Father, I love you. You have forgiven me of my sins and given me a new life in Christ. You do all things well. I trust you. I make the decision today to surrender my finances to you. I choose not to serve money any longer. I'm not sure yet what it means but I trust you. Have your way in my finances. Amen.

ATTRIBUTE SEVEN · STEP THREE
MANAGE YOUR BODY

Scripture Memory:

"But_____ _____ his _____ and ___ _____ , and ___
these things_____ __ _____ to you as _____." Matthew__:33

"But seek first his kingdom and his righteousness, and all these things will be given to you as well." Matthew 6:33

Read: Deuteronomy 6:5; Genesis 1:26–31

GENESIS 1:26–31 CAN HELP YOU REALIGN YOUR LIFE and how you view your body. There are three things you must understand from these verses. First, God created you. You are not self-made. You did not evolve over a long period of time from an earlier life form. There is a personal, Creator God who designed you. You are different from anyone who has ever been on this earth. Second, you are made in God's image. This means you are uniquely designed to partner with God as his representative in your world for this time in history. You were not designed to do your own thing. To get the third point, you need to reread Genesis 1:31. What did God think about the humans he had made on the sixth day?..

If you look back over Genesis 1 at the end of the other five days, you will see that God said, "It was good." It was only after he made humans that God said, "It was *very* good" (emphasis mine). When God looks at you, he sees a masterpiece. The mass media has taught us to compare ourselves to others and to devalue certain aspects of our bodies that are not like someone else's. That is not God's perspective. He made each person different and special. If you are going to become who God has designed you to be, you must allow his thoughts about you to rule. Your body is "very good." You will find great freedom when you look at your body and your life from God's point of view. Why not begin by praying Psalm 139:13–16:

> For you (God) created my inmost being; you knit me together in my mother's womb. I praise you because I am fearfully and wonderfully made; your works are wonderful, I know that full well. My frame was not hidden from you when I was made in the secret place, when I was woven together in the depths of the earth. Your eyes saw my unformed body; all the days ordained for me were written in your book before one of them came to be.

Thanking God for your body and accepting God's view of your body are essential for your walk with God. It is also essential that you accept his purpose for your body, to partner with God for his purpose.

Several Scriptures will help shape how you think about your body. First, Deuteronomy 6:5 describes what you do with your body as worship: "Love the LORD your God with all your heart and with all your soul and with all your strength." Worship is not just what you do on Sunday during a service. Everything you do with your body is an act of worship to God or worship of yourself. In practical terms, what you eat, how much or how little you eat, how much you sleep, what you drink, how and with whom you enjoy sex, how you work, whom you serve and the like, are all matters of worship, ways of expressing your love to God. If you view your body as an instrument to please yourself, you will do your own thing, what feels good or seems right to you. If you know your body is a gift from God for which you are responsible to him, you will use it to worship him and to bring him honor. Romans 12:1 describes it this way: "Therefore, I urge you, brothers and sisters, in view of God's mercy, to offer your bodies as a living sacrifice, holy and pleasing to God—this is your true and proper worship." Embracing this view of your body will change everything. What comes to your mind right now that you will need to adjust based on the truth of this principle?

Sometimes when it comes to these kinds of things, people feel like they are going to miss out on a lot of fun. There is no doubt there will be short-term pleasures you will bypass if you offer your body to God. While temporary pleasures like overeating, over drinking, and having sex outside of a monogamous marriage seem to be fun, in the end they produce much pain and disappointment. Overeating results in all kinds of health problems. Alcoholism and drug abuse destroy bodies and families, and they steal valuable resources that could be used to invest in the future. Sex outside of marriage is always destructive. 1 Corinthians 6:18–20 describes it this way:

> Flee from sexual immorality. All other sins a person commits are outside the body, but whoever sins sexually, sins against their own body. Do you not know that your bodies are temples of the Holy Spirit, who is in you, whom you have received from God? You are not your own; you were bought at a price. Therefore honor God with your bodies.

God's ways are always best. Romans 6:12–13 describes the choice you have with your body now that you know the Lord:

> Therefore do not let sin reign in your mortal body so that you obey its evil desires. 13 Do not offer any part of yourself to sin as an instrument of wickedness, but rather offer yourselves to

God as those who have been brought from death to life; and offer every part of yourself to him as an instrument of righteousness.

Adjusting what you do with your body is a process. Most people have to start in one area and then move to another. What aspects of what you do with your body need adjustment? ....

....

....

You will want to prioritize these and strategize with your spiritual coach about what your next decisions need to be.

Prayer:
Heavenly Father, thank you for my body. I praise you because I am fearfully and wonderfully made. I haven't thought that way about my body until now. Thank you for accepting me and loving me just like I am. Thank you for showing me how much you value my body; you bought me with a precious price. I accept as truth that my body is "very good." I offer my body back to you as an instrument of righteousness. May what I do with my body honor you from this day forward. I need your help as I learn how to do that. Amen.

ATTRIBUTE SEVEN · STEP FOUR
MANAGE YOUR WORDS

Scripture Memory:

"But ____ first ____ _____ and ____ _____ , and __
____ ____ __ __ _____ to ____ as ____." Matthew 6: __

"But seek first his kingdom and his righteousness, and all these things will be given to you as well." Matthew 6:33

Read: James 3:3–12; Matthew 12:33–37; Ephesians 4:29–32

WHEN I WAS A CHILD and someone would say something hurtful, I would often hear my friends say, "Sticks and stones may break my bones but words can never hurt me." We all knew it wasn't true, but they would say it anyway in hopes that the person would stop saying the hurtful things. Words are powerful. We all know it.

What analogies does James use to describe the power of the tongue? ....

Powerful communication can serve as a rudder to motivate a large group of people to go in a certain direction. It can also destroy lots of people like a spark can destroy a forest. Words are powerful. As a follower of Jesus, your words must become those which turn people to Christ. You may have struggled with your words up till now. Perhaps you have said hurtful things to others or even to yourself. Maybe you gossiped about someone or told a story in a way that made someone look bad. I know I have. As you follow Christ, he will show you how your words can be life-giving.

People do a variety of things to deal with the problem of the tongue. Some people opt to not talk much, just to stuff it. This is not a bad option because it keeps you from saying things you would regret later. Others say things and then try to retract them by saying, "I am sorry I said that. I really didn't mean it. I was just angry." Still others don't worry too much about it. They just say what's on their mind and they let others deal with it. They are proud that people say of them, "You always know where you stand with that person. He speaks his mind." Each of these has their benefits but none of these are the way of Jesus. Let's look at the passages you read today.

According to James 3:5–6, what does the tongue do?

All three of the responses mentioned above are our attempts to tame our own tongue. What does James 3:8 say about these approaches to the tongue?

According to Jesus' words in Matthew 12:33–35, what is the core issue?

It really is a heart issue, isn't it? What comes out of you and me is what is really in us. If Christ fills us with good things and removes the bad things in our hearts, our speech will follow because it is out of the overflow of the heart that our mouths speak. If your heart is full of good things, when it overflows, good things will come out. If it is full of evil things, evil things will come out. Think of your tongue as a barometer of your heart. What you talk about and think about is what is important to you. Listen to yourself talk today. What kinds of things do you talk about? You may want to keep a notepad near you today to monitor your thoughts and words. Your words will indicate what you value and the condition of your soul. When you hear yourself saying something you think would not glorify God, ask yourself why you are saying it. Is it because you want others to perceive you a certain way? Are you trying to get someone to do something?

Allowing Jesus to transform your heart and your words is extremely important because Jesus says in Matthew 12:36–37 that we will have to give account one day for every word we said. We are responsible for our hearts and our words. That's a sobering thought. What better time than now to surrender your heart and words to the Lord?

What strategies does the Apostle Paul give in Ephesians 4:29–32 that could help you with your heart and words?

If you are going to honor Christ with your tongue, you have to make a concerted effort in five ways. First, even though you cannot tame your tongue, you can curb what you say that is hurtful (Ephesians 4:29). You have probably heard the saying, "If you don't have something good to say, don't say it." There is some truth to this. You can develop the habit of saying only good things about others. Second, you need to acknowledge that it grieves the Holy Spirit when you say hurtful things about others (Ephesians 4:30). God loves everyone, and it hurts him when you talk poorly about the ones he created. Third, you must get rid of bitterness, rage, anger, brawling, slander and malice (Ephesians 4:31). Most of the time we say hurtful things about people who have hurt us. When you want to say something hurtful about someone, ask yourself how that person hurt you. When you identify that hurt, take it to the Lord. You may want to go back to Attribute Six–Step 4 of this guide to remind yourself how to pray through pain. Let God carry the pain for you. Let it go. Get rid of it. Fourth, be kind and compassionate to others (Ephesians 6:32). Regardless of how others treat you, you have control over your actions towards them. There is great freedom in knowing someone's actions do not dictate your responses. You can be kind and compassionate towards others because God is that way to you. Fifth, we all need forgiveness. The pathway to learning to love God with your words comes back to God's forgiveness for you. When you remember how much you needed and still need God to forgive you, it enables you to forgive others.

What would you like to do today to apply these principles to your life? ....
....
....

Prayer:

Tell God in your own words what you would like him to help you with today. Be sure to thank him for what he has done in your life already.

ATTRIBUTE SEVEN · STEP FIVE
MANAGE YOUR TIME

Scripture Memory:

"___ ___ ___ ___ ___ ___ ___ ___ ___ ___ ___ , ___ ___
___ ___ ___ ___ ___ ___ ___ ___ . " ___ : ___

"But seek first his kingdom and his righteousness, and all these things will be given to you as well." Matthew 6:33

Read: Genesis 2:2–3; Exodus 20:8–11; Genesis 2:15; Psalm 90:12; Ecclesiastes 3

Leo Tolstoy wrote a famous story entitled, "How Much Land Does a Man Need?"[1] In it he describes an ambitious peasant named Pakhom, who heard about a country where he could have all the land he wanted for a thousand rubles. The only requirement was that he had to be able to walk around the entire plot in one day. Pakhom was quite confident that he could go far in one day. The rules were simple. He paid the thousand rubles upfront, would walk the entire property in one day, and then return to the starting point by sundown. If he did not get back to the starting point by sundown, the money and the land would be forfeited. In the story, Pakhom went too far in the early part of the day which resulted in his having to push himself especially hard to try to get back to the starting point. Near the end of the day the story describes him running with burning lungs, a sweat-soaked shirt and a parched throat. He did make it back to the starting point just in time and he collapsed. Pakhom's worker ran to help him up only to discover he had died of exhaustion. The worker took Pakhom's shovel, dug a grave, and buried him on a six-foot piece of land, the exact amount of land a man needs.

Many of us are running ourselves ragged by living overloaded lives. Our lust for more is driving us to live beyond our limits, and it is resulting in exhaustion and burnout. God did not design us to work or play all the time. He designed us to work hard for short seasons and then to rest and reflect.

God set aside one day a week for rest and renewal. Read Genesis 2:2–3 again. Does it surprise you that God rested from his work? Why or why not?

I believe God rested on the seventh day not because he was tired but to model for us that we need it.

God's ways are always best but we don't always think so. Notice in Exodus 20:7–11 that taking a Sabbath is one of the Ten Commandments. God requires it of his people.

Why do you think most Americans do not take a day to rest and reflect?

Do you currently take a day to rest and reflect? Why or why not?

Some people start obeying God in this area by taking a portion of a day to rest and reflect and then grow into it. Others just dive right in and take twenty-four hours. Would you like to work towards taking a Sabbath (one day to rest) or a portion of a Sabbath?

What kinds of things could you do on a Sabbath to help you renew your spiritual, physical, and emotional being?

What decisions would you need to make for that to happen?

What will you have to give up?

Choosing to not work when you are able is equally dishonoring to God. Notice in Genesis 2:15 that God gave man work before the curse. In other words, work is not part of the curse. Work is harder because of the curse but work is not the curse. This means it is God's will that you would embrace your work in life. The Bible describes those who do not work faithfully as "sluggards." There are painful consequences for living the life of a sluggard which you will want to avoid.[2] The Apostle Paul wrote directly to men in 1 Timothy 5:8 about providing for their families, "Anyone who does not provide for their relatives, and especially for their own household, has denied the faith and is worse than an unbeliever."

Is working a problem for you?

If so, what step are you going to take to change this?

Learning to be a good manager of your time is all about balance, making sure you are taking care of the most important things first. A good start is to establish times when you work and rest and reflect. We could have also talked about making time for important relationships, taking care of your body, et cetera. It is a process to learn how to use your time to honor God.

Are there other areas of your life that you need God's help with concerning your time?

What needs to happen so you can take steps in the right direction? ....
....

You will want to share your decisions with your spiritual coach.

How about asking God to help you right now by praying Psalm 90:12 with the psalmist?

> ### *Prayer:*
> Lord, teach me to number my days aright, that I may gain a heart of wisdom. I want to please you with how I manage my time. Help me as I take steps today to be faithful with the time you have given me. I want to honor you and fulfill my purpose. I believe I can do that if you will help me and guide me. Amen.

ATTRIBUTE SEVEN · STEP SIX
MANAGE YOUR GIFTS

Scripture Memory:

"_____ _____ _____ _____ _____ _____ , __ __ __

_____ _____ _____ _____ _____ _____ ." _____ : __

"But seek first his kingdom and his righteousness, and all these things will be given to you as well." Matthew 6:33

Read: Ephesians 2:10; 1 Corinthians 12:7–11; 1 Peter 4:10–11; Matthew 25:14–30

IT IS AN AMAZING THING TO ME THAT GOD ALLOWS us the privilege of joining with him to change the world. He could do everything himself, but he chooses to do some of his work through us. I am so humbled by that.

How does Ephesians 2:10 describe us? ....

Why were we created? ....
When did God prepare our work for us? ....

You are not an accident or an evolution of nature. God had you in mind long before you were born. He designed you with specific spiritual gifts, passions, abilities, and a certain personality type so you could make a unique impact on the world that would bring him glory. Isn't that affirming? You may not know at this point what your unique contribution will be for God, but the Bible assures you that God has a plan for your life that is unlike anyone else's.

According to 1 Corinthians 12:7, to whom does the Spirit give gifts?

Why were these gifts given?

It is really important to realize the gifts God gives you are not for you but for others. No one has all the gifts. That's why we need one another to become all that God wants us to become. When I do my part and you do yours, we can make an impact for God.

According to 1 Corinthians 12:11, who decides who receives which gifts?

How does 1 Peter 4:10 affect how you think about your gifts?

According to 1 Peter 4:11, what is the ultimate goal of your gifts?

I would not be telling you the whole truth if I didn't tell you there are huge implications for how you manage the gifts God has given you. Matthew 25:14–30 describes God's kingdom like a master who entrusted his property to his servants before he went on a journey. He gave each of them a different portion of his property (called "talents" in the story). When he returned, he expected each of them to have done something with the resources he gave them. Those who received five and two talents used them to gain even more. This pleased the master and he put them in charge of many things. But the servant who received only one talent and did nothing with it, received a harsh rebuke from the master. The master said, "You wicked, lazy servant." And the master took what he had given to that servant, and he gave it away to those who had done something with their resources. Then the master cast the servant out into the darkness where there was weeping and gnashing of teeth. This is a sobering parable but one we should take to heart as followers of Jesus. God invests heavily in each one of us because he has significant purposes for our lives. His purpose for your life is important. You only fail if you attempt nothing for God.

What gifts and resources has God given you?

....

....

What would you like to do for God if you knew he would bless it?

....

....

What could you do with what God has given you to serve others?

....

....

....

As we conclude *Follow: Learning to Follow Jesus*, I want to pray for us.

Prayer:

It amazes me, Heavenly Father, that you reach out to us to show us your kindness, to love us, to teach us, to befriend us, and to give us a meaningful life. It humbles me to realize that our lives matter so much to you. Help us to manage the gifts and resources you have given us in such a way that we fulfill what you had in mind when you created us. Help us to live today and each day hereafter for you alone. Thank you for giving our lives meaning. We belong to you. Amen.

ATTRIBUTE SEVEN

DECISIONS

RESOURCES

• • •

ATTRIBUTE ONE · LEARN TO BE WITH JESUS

• • •

HOW TO DEVELOP A SCHEDULE

1. **Values**
   - → The values of the follower of Jesus are two-fold: loving God and loving people.

2. **Roles**
   - → God has given you specific roles (steward, husband, father, friend, et cetera) and resources to manage (time, talent, energy, and money).

3. **Tasks**
   - → Make a list of tasks you perform under each role.

4. **Time**
   - → Estimate the amount of time each task will take on a weekly basis so that Christ is honored.
   - → Add up the hours and subtract the total from 168.

5. **Analysis**
   - → Set aside time weekly to evaluate and plan how you will spend your time based on your values.

6. **Plot** the hours on a weekly schedule.

Sample Time Analysis

	Wkly Hrs	Total
1. LOVER OF GOD (130 hours)		
a. Steward—Spiritual Formation		14
i. Quiet time—0.5 hours x 7 days	3.5	
ii. Corporate Worship Service	2.5	
iii. Small Group/with dinner	3	
iv. Spiritual Coaching	2	
v. Ministry Involvement	3	
b. Steward—Physical, Emotional, Mental		66
i. Sleep (7 hours)	49	
ii. Eating (Breakfast .5; Lunch .5)	7	
iii. Personal hygiene (.5 daily)	3.5	
iv. Workout—Cardio	3	
v. Reading	2	
vi. Weekly planning	1.5	
c. Steward - Employment		50
i. Work	45	
ii. Commuting Time	5	
2. LOVER OF PEOPLE (30 hours)		
a. As a Husband		10
i. Personal Time	7	
ii. Household Chores	3	
b. As a Father		16
i. Dinner	6	
ii. Family Time	7	
iii. Family Night	3	
c. As a Friend, Family Member, and Neighbor		4
i. Neighbors	1	
ii. Friendship with a pre-Christian	1	
iii. Extended family	2	
TOTAL HOURS		160
TOTAL HOURS IN A WEEK		168
TOTAL WEEKLY DISCRETIONARY TIME		8

ATTRIBUTE TWO · LEARN TO LISTEN

● ● ●

BIBLE STUDY PROCESS

Choose a **Passage** (usually a paragraph) of Scripture you would like to study (I recommend starting with Philippians 4:4–7).

Step 1—Read through the entire **Book** in which your passage occurs in no more than two sittings. Take note of what stands out to you. What questions do you have as you read the book?

Step 2—Reread the entire **Book** looking for clues to the following questions: Who wrote the book? To whom did he write? What kinds of issues were important to the recipients? Are there any clues in the book as to when the letter was written? Why was the book written? What are the natural or logical divisions of the book?

Step 3—Read what others say about the 5 questions in Bible dictionaries, Bible encyclopedias, Bible handbooks, commentaries, and introductions.

Step 4—Identify the **Section** of the book in which your **Passage** occurs. (A **Section** is a group of **Passages** [paragraphs] that have the same focus.) Read the **Section** twice and identify the following:
1. The main focus of your **Section** in one sentence.
2. How each **Passage** advances the main focus of your **Section**.

Step 5—Read your **Passage** 3 times. List as many observations as you can about your **Passage** using the six observation questions to guide you: What is emphasized? What is repeated? What is related? What is alike? What is unlike? What is true to life?

Step 6—Read your **Passage** in 4 different translations and look up all marginal references in your passage.

Step 7—Identify, research, and explain every historical context item in your **Passage**.

Step 8—Do the following steps for every significant word in your **Passage**:

1. Where does this word occur in the passage? First sentence? Last?
2. Is the word repeated in the passage? If so, how many times and in which verse(s)?
3. At first glance what do you think this word means in this passage?
4. Using a concordance, make a list of every reference to your word in the book you are studying.
5. Look up and read every reference to the word in the book. (Note: if the word is used more than 25–30 times in the book, look up primarily those which fall in your section and others which seem to be significant throughout the book.)
6. Write a short phrase beside each reference to help you remember the context. (Note: if you are studying a verb, include who is speaking or doing the action and to whom. In what context is the action taking place? If you are studying a noun, what is this thing used for? If it is a place, what happens there?)
7. Is this word used in similar contexts? What is that context?
8. Does the word occur primarily in one section or passage of the book?
9. Read about your word from theological wordbooks and commentaries.

10.How does the meaning of this word clarify the meaning of the sentence in the passage in the section in the book you are studying?

Step 9—Develop a one-sentence statement that includes the main idea of the **Passage** and what it meant to the original audience.

Step 10—Develop a one sentence teaching statement that summarizes what the **Passage** means for all people. How will people's lives change if they get the main point of this passage? What will people think, feel, and do if they get the point?

ATTRIBUTE THREE · LEARN TO HEAL

● ● ●

CONFLICT RESOLUTION PROCESS[1]

Overview of Conflict
1. It is a normal part of life.
2. Provides an opportunity to grow.
3. We decide how we are going to handle conflict.

Problem Solving Process
1. Pray to get your own heart right before you do anything.
   → Do not proceed until you know before God that you love the other person and want God's best for them.
2. Set a time and place for discussion
   → Make sure you set aside adequate time.
   → Choose a place to talk where you will not be interrupted.
3. Define the problem or issue of disagreement.
   → Select one issue at a time.

→ Define the issue in a way that is mutually agreeable.

4. How do each of you contribute to the problem?
   → The purpose is to discover how the problem evolved in order to find a solution.
5. List past attempts to resolve the issue that were not successful.
6. Brainstorm about possible solutions.
   → The purpose of this is to generate fresh ideas without attempting to evaluate their relative merits.
7. Discuss and evaluate the possible solutions.
8. Agree on one solution and try.
   → To agree upon a choice does not always mean it is the first choice of either partner.
9. Agree on how each individual will work toward this solution.
   → Be specific and focus on observable behaviors.
10. Set up another meeting to discuss your progress.
    → Set the meeting reasonably soon (i.e., one week from now).
    → Partners can discuss the degree to which the plan is working and in which to further their progress.
11. Reward each other as you each contribute toward the solution.
    → Watch for ways in which your partner positively contributes to resolving the conflict.
    → Encourage and praise one another for their efforts.

GRIEF PROCESS[2]

1. **Shock stage:** Initial paralysis at hearing the bad news.
2. **Denial stage:** Frustrated outpouring of bottled-up emotion.

3. **Bargaining stage:** Seeking in vain for a way out.
4. **Depression stage:** Final realization of the inevitable.
5. **Testing stage:** Seeking realistic solutions.
6. **Acceptance stage:** Finally finding the way forward.

12 STEP RECOVERY PROCESS WITH SCRIPTURE REFERENCES[3]

Step 1 We admitted we were powerless over our addictions and compulsive behaviors, that our lives had become unmanageable.

> I know that nothing good lives in me, that is, in my sinful nature. For I have the desire to do what is good, but I cannot carry it out. Romans 7:18

Step 2 We came to believe that a power greater than ourselves could restore us to sanity.

> For it is God who works in you to will and to act according to his good purpose. Philippians 2:13

Step 3 We made a decision to turn our lives and our wills over to the care of God.

> Therefore, I urge you, brothers, in view of God's mercy, to offer your bodies as living sacrifices, holy and pleasing to God—this is your spiritual act of worship. Romans 12:1

Step 4 We made a searching and fearless moral inventory of ourselves.

> Let us examine our ways and test them, and let us return to the Lord. Lamentations 3:40

Step 5 We admitted to God, to ourselves, and to another human being the exact nature of our wrongs.

> Therefore confess your sins to each other and pray for each other so that you may be healed. James 5:16

Step 6 We were entirely ready to have God remove all these defects of character.

> Humble yourselves before the Lord, and he will lift you up. James 4:10

Step 7 We humbly asked Him to remove all our shortcomings.

> If we confess our sins, he is faithful and just and will forgive us our sins and purify us from all unrighteousness. 1 John 1:9

Step 8 We made a list of all persons we had harmed and became willing to make amends to them all.

> Do to others as you would have them do to you. Luke 6:31

Step 9 We made direct amends to such people whenever possible, except when to do so would injure them or others.

> Therefore, if you are offering your gift at the altar and there remember that your brother has something against you, leave your gift there in front of the altar. First go and be reconciled to your brother; then come and offer your gift. Matthew 5:23–24

Step 10 We continue to take personal inventory and when we were wrong, promptly admitted it.

> So, if you think you are standing firm, be careful that you don't fall! 1 Corinthians 10:12

Step 11 We sought through prayer and meditation to improve our conscious contact with God, praying only for knowledge of his will for us, and power to carry that out.

> Let the word of Christ dwell in you richly. Colossians 3:16

Step 12 Having had a spiritual experience as the result of these steps, we try to carry this message to others and to practice these principles in all our affairs.

> Brothers, if someone is caught in a sin, you who are spiritual should restore him gently. But watch yourself, or you also may be tempted. Galatians 6:1

ATTRIBUTE FOUR · LEARN TO INFLUENCE

● ● ●

EVANGELISM STYLES QUESTIONNAIRE[1]

Directions

1. Record your response to each of the 36 statements according to whether you think that statement applies to you:

3	2	1	0
Very much	Somewhat	Very little	Not at all

2. Transfer your responses to the grid at the bottom of page 226 and total each column.

........1.   In conversations, I like to approach topics directly, without much small talk or beating around the bush.

........2.   I have a hard time getting out of bookstores or libraries without getting a bunch of books that will help me better understand issues being debated in society.

........3.   I often tell stories about my personal experiences in order to illustrate a point I am trying to make.

........4.   I am a "people person" who places a high value on friendship.

........5.   I enjoy including or adding new people to activities in which I am involved.

........6.   I see needs in people's lives that others often overlook.

........7.   I do not shy away from putting a person on the spot when it seems necessary.

........8.   I tend to be analytical.

........9.   I often identify with others by using phrases like "I used to think that too" or "I once felt the way you do."

......10.   Other people have commented about my ability for developing new friendships.

......11.   To be honest, even if I know the answers, I am more comfortable having someone "better qualified" explain Christianity to my friends.

......12.   I find fulfillment in helping others, often in behind-the-scenes ways.

13. I do not have a problem confronting my friends with the truth even if it risks hurting the relationship.

14. In conversations, I naturally focus on the questions that are holding up a person's spiritual progress.

15. When I tell people how I came to Christ, I have found that they have been interested in hearing it.

16. I would rather delve into personal life issues than abstract theological ideas.

17. If I knew of a high quality outreach event that my friends would enjoy, I would make a big effort to bring them.

18. I prefer to show love through my actions more than my words.

19. I believe that real love often means telling someone the truth, even when it hurts.

20. I enjoy discussions and debates on difficult questions.

21. I intentionally share my mistakes with others when it will help them relate to the solutions I have found.

22. I prefer getting involved in discussions concerning a person's life before dealing with the details of their beliefs.

23. I tend to watch for spiritually strategic events to bring people to (such as Christian concerts, outreach events, seeker services).

24. When people are spiritually closed, I have found that my quiet demonstrations of Christian love sometimes make them more receptive.

25. A motto that would fit me is: "Make a difference or a mess, but do something."

26. I often get frustrated with people when they use weak arguments or poor logic.

27. People seem interested in hearing stories about things that have happened in my life.

28. I enjoy long talks with friends.

29. I am always looking for a match between the needs and interests of my friends and the various events, books, etc., that they would enjoy or from which they would benefit.

30. I feel more comfortable physically assisting a person in the name of Christ than getting involved in religious discussions.

...... 31. I sometimes get in trouble for lacking gentleness and sensitivity in the way I interact with others.

...... 32. I like to get at the underlying reasons for opinions people hold.

...... 33. I am still amazed at how God brought me to faith in Him and I am motivated to tell people about it.

...... 34. People generally consider me to be an interactive, sensitive, and caring kind of person.

...... 35. A highlight of my week would be to take a guest with me to an appropriate church event.

...... 36. I tend to be more practical and action-oriented than philosophical and idea-oriented.

	Confrontational	Intellectual	Testimonial	Interpersonal	Invitational	Serving
	#1 ___	#2 ___	#3 ___	#4 ___	#5 ___	#6 ___
	#7 ___	#8 ___	#9 ___	#10 ___	#11 ___	#12 ___
	#13 ___	#14 ___	#15 ___	#16 ___	#17 ___	#18 ___
	#19 ___	#20 ___	#21 ___	#22 ___	#23 ___	#24 ___
	#25 ___	#26 ___	#27 ___	#28 ___	#29 ___	#30 ___
	#31 ___	#32 ___	#33 ___	#34 ___	#35 ___	#36 ___
TOTALS						

Evangelism Style Examples & Summaries

Confrontational Style—Acts 2—Peter, Billy Graham, Chuck Colson
> ⤍ Characteristics: Confident, Assertive, Direct
> ⤍ Cautions: Be sure to use tact when confronting people with truth to keep them from becoming unnecessarily offended.

Intellectual Style—Acts 17—Paul, Josh McDowell, D. James Kennedy, Alpha Course

⟶ Characteristics: Inquisitive, Analytical, Logical

⟶ Cautions: Do not substitute giving answers for giving the Gospel message. Be careful of becoming argumentative.

Testimonial Style—John 9:25—Blind man, Corrie ten Boom, Joni Erickson Tada

⟶ Characteristics: Clear Communicator, Story Teller, Good Listener

⟶ Cautions: Beware of talking about yourself but not relating your experience to the other person's life. You first need to listen to them to be able to connect your story to their situation.

Interpersonal Style—Luke 5:29—Matthew, Becky Pippert, Joe Aldrich

⟶ Characteristics: Warm Personality, Conversational, Friendship-Oriented

⟶ Cautions: Avoid valuing friendship over truth-telling. Presenting the Gospel often means challenging a person's whole direction in life, and that can mean causing friction in your relationship.

Invitational Style—John 1:42, 46—Andrew & Philip, woman at the well in John 4, Ruth Graham

⟶ Characteristics: Hospitable, Relational, Persuasive

⟶ Cautions: Be careful not to always let others do your talking for you. You too, need to "always be prepared to give an answer to everyone who asks you to give the reason for the hope that you have…" (1 Peter 3:15)

Serving Style—Acts 9—Dorcas, Mother Teresa

⟶ Characteristics: Others-Centered, Humble, Patient

⟶ Cautions: Just as "words are no substitute for actions," "actions are no substitute for words." In Romans 10:14, it is made clear that we verbally tell people about Christ.

ATTRIBUTE FIVE · LEARN TO LOVE

• • •

STEP I—TRUSTING GOD ASSESSMENT[1]

Instructions

1. Read each of the following statements and put the appropriate number of the term that best describes you.

2. Add up the total number for each section.

3. Read the interpretation of your score that is found on the next page.

1	2	3	4	5	6	7
Always	Very Often	Often	Sometimes	Seldom	Very Seldom	Never

........1. Because of fear, I often avoid participating in certain activities.

........2. When I sense that I might experience failure in some important area, I become nervous and anxious.

........3. I worry.

........4. I have unexplained anxiety.

........5. I am a perfectionist.

........6. I am compelled to justify my mistakes.

........7. There are certain areas in which I feel I *must* succeed.

........8. I become depressed when I fail.

........9. I am angry with people who interfere with my attempts to succeed, and as a result, make me appear incompetent.

........10. I am self-critical.

........TOTAL (See next page for analysis.)

Trusting God versus Fear of Failure

If your score is...

57–70: God has apparently given you a very strong appreciation for His love and unconditional acceptance. You seem to be freed from the fear of failure that plagues most people. (Some people who score this high are either greatly deceived, or have become callous to their emotions as a way to suppress pain.)

47–56: The fear of failure controls your responses rarely, or only in certain situations. Again, the only major exceptions are those who are not honest with themselves.

37–46: When you experience emotional problems, they may relate to a sense of failure or to some form of criticism. Upon reflection, you will probably relate many of your previous decisions to this fear. Many of your future decisions will also be affected by the fear of failure unless you take direct action to overcome it.

27–36: The fear of failure forms a general backdrop to your life. There are probably few days that you are not affected in some way by this fear. Unfortunately, this robs you of the joy and peace your salvation is meant to bring.

0–26: Experiences of failure dominate your memory, and have probably resulted in a great deal of depression. These problems will remain until some definitive action is taken. In other words, this condition will not simply disappear; time alone cannot heal your pain. You need to experience deep healing in your self-concept, in your relationship with God, and in your relationships with others.

STEP 2—SEEKING GOD ASSESSMENT[2]
Instructions

1. Read each of the following statements and put the appropriate number of the term that best describes you.

2. Add up the total number for each section.

3. Read the interpretation of your score that is found on the next page.

1	2	3	4	5	6	7
Always	Very Often	Often	Sometimes	Seldom	Very Seldom	Never

.........1. I avoid certain people.

.........2. When I sense that someone might reject me, I become nervous and anxious.

.........3. I am uncomfortable around those who are different from me.

.........4. It bothers me when someone is unfriendly to me.

.........5. I am basically shy and unsocial.

.........6. I am critical of others.

.........7. I find myself trying to impress others.

.........8. I become depressed when someone criticizes me.

.........9. I always try to determine what people think of me.

.......10. I don't understand people and what motivates them.

.........TOTAL (See next page for analysis.)

Seeking God's Approval versus Fear of Rejection

If your score is...

57–70: God has apparently given you a very strong appreciation for His love and unconditional acceptance. You seem to be freed from the fear of rejection that plagues most people. (Some people who score this high are either greatly deceived, or have become callous to their emotions as a way to suppress pain.)

47–56: The fear of rejection controls your responses rarely, or only in certain situations. Again, the only major exceptions are those who are not honest with themselves.

37–46: When you experience emotional problems, they may relate to a sense of rejection. Upon reflection, you will probably relate many of your previous decisions to this fear. Many of your future decisions will also be affected by the fear of rejection unless you take direct action to overcome it.

27–36: The fear of rejection forms a general backdrop to your life. There are probably few days that you are not affected in some way by this fear. Unfortunately, this robs you of the joy and peace your salvation is meant to bring.

0–26: Experiences of rejection dominate your memory, and have probably resulted in a great deal of depression. These problems will persist until some definitive action is taken. In other words, this condition will not simply disappear; time alone cannot heal your pain. You need to experience deep healing in your self-concept, in your relationship with God, and in your relationships with others.

STEP 3—ENJOYING GOD'S ACCEPTANCE ASSESSMENT[3]

Instructions

1. Read each of the following statements and put the appropriate number of the term that best describes you.

2. Add up the total number for each section.

3. Read the interpretation of your score that is found on the next page.

1	2	3	4	5	6	7
Always	Very Often	Often	Sometimes	Seldom	Very Seldom	Never

........1. I fear what God might do to me.

........2. After I fail, I worry about God's response.

........3. When I see someone in a difficult situation, I wonder what he or she did to deserve it.

........4. When something goes wrong, I have a tendency to think that God must be punishing me.

........5. I am very hard on myself when I fail.

........6. I find myself wanting to blame people when they fail.

........7. I get angry with God when someone who is immoral or dishonest prospers.

........8. I am compelled to tell others when I see them doing wrong.

........9. I tend to focus on the faults and failures of others.

......10. God seems harsh to me.

.......TOTAL (See next page for analysis.)

Enjoying God's Acceptance versus Fear of Punishment

If your score is...

57–70: God has apparently given you a very strong appreciation for His unconditional love and acceptance. You seem to be freed from the fear of punishment that plagues most people. (Some people who score this high are either greatly deceived, or have become callous to their emotions as a way to suppress pain.)

47–56: The fear of punishment and the compulsion to punish others controls your responses rarely, or only in certain situations. Again, the only major exceptions are those who are not honest with themselves.

37–46: When you experience emotional problems, they may relate to a fear of punishment or to an inner urge to punish others. Upon reflection, you will probably relate many of your previous decisions to this fear. Many of your future decisions will also be affected by the fear of punishment and/or the compulsion to punish others unless you take direct action to overcome these tendencies.

27–36: The fear of punishment forms a general backdrop to your life. There are probably few days that you are not affected in some way by the fear of punishment and the propensity to blame others. Unfortunately, this robs you of the joy and peace your salvation is meant to bring.

0–26: Experiences of punishment dominate your memory, and you probably have suffered a great deal of depression as a result of them. These problems will remain until some definitive plan is followed. In other words, this condition will not simply disappear; time alone cannot heal your pain. You need to experience deep healing in your self-concept, in your relationship with God, and in your relationships with others.

STEP 4—PARTNERING WITH GOD TO CHANGE YOU ASSESSMENT[4]

Instructions

1. Read each of the following statements and put the appropriate number of the term that best describes you.

2. Add up the total number for each section.

3. Read the interpretation of your score that is found on the next page.

1	2	3	4	5	6	7
Always	Very Often	Often	Sometimes	Seldom	Very Seldom	Never

...... 1. I often think about past failures or experiences of rejection.

...... 2. There are certain things about my past which I cannot recall without experiencing strong, painful emotions (i.e. guilt, shame, anger, fear, etc.).

...... 3. I seem to make the same mistakes over and over again.

...... 4. There are certain aspects of my character that I want to change, but I don't believe I can ever successfully do so.

...... 5. I feel inferior.

...... 6. There are aspects of my appearance that I cannot accept.

...... 7. I am generally disgusted with myself.

...... 8. I feel that certain experiences have basically ruined my life.

...... 9. I perceive of myself as an immoral person.

...... 10. I feel that I have lost the opportunity to experience a complete and wonderful life.

...... TOTAL (See next page for analysis.)

Partnering with God for Change versus Fear of Shame

If your score is...

57–70: God has apparently given you a very strong appreciation for His love and unconditional acceptance. You seem to be freed from the shame that plagues most people. (Some people who score this high are either greatly deceived, or have become callous to their emotions as a way to suppress pain.)

47–56: Shame controls your responses rarely, or only in certain situations. Again, the exceptions are those who are not honest with themselves.

37–46: When you experience emotional problems, they may relate to a sense of shame. Upon reflection, you will probably relate many of your previous decisions to feelings of worthlessness. Many of your future decisions will also be affected by low self-esteem unless you take direct action to overcome it.

27–36: Shame forms a generally negative backdrop to your life. There are probably few days that you are not affected in some way by shame. Unfortunately, this robs you of the joy and peace your salvation was meant to bring.

0–26: Experiences of shame dominate your memory, and have probably resulted in a great deal of depression. These problems will persist until some definitive action is taken. In other words, this condition will not simply disappear one day; time alone cannot heal your pain. You need to experience deep healing in your self-concept, in your relationship with God, and in your relationships with others.

GOD'S ANSWER FOR FOUR COMMON LIES[5]

Lie	False Beliefs
The Performance Trap	I must meet certain standards in order to feel good about myself.
Approval Addict	I must be approved (accepted) by certain others to feel good about myself.
The Blame Game	Those who fail are unworthy of love and deserve to be punished.
Shame	I am what I am. I cannot change. I am hopeless.

Consequences	God's Answer
The fear of failure; perfectionism; driven to succeed; manipulating others to achieve success; withdrawal from risks.	**Justification** Justification means that God has not only forgiven me of my sins, but also has granted me the righteousness of Christ. Because of justification, I bear Christ's righteousness and am, therefore, fully pleasing to the Father (Rom. 5:1).
The fear of rejection; attempting to please others at any cost; overly sensitive to criticism; withdrawing from others to avoid disapproval.	**Reconciliation** Reconciliation means that although I was at one time hostile toward God and alienated from Him, I am now forgiven and have been brought into an intimate relationship with Him. Consequently, I am totally accepted by God (Col. 1:21–22).
The fear of punishment; punishing others; blaming others for personal failure; withdrawal from God and others; driven to avoid failure.	**Propitiation** Propitiation means that Christ satisfied God's wrath by His death on the cross; therefore, I am deeply loved by God (1 John 4:9–11).
Feelings of shame, hopelessness, inferiority; passivity; loss of creativity; isolation; withdrawal from others.	**Regeneration** Regeneration means that I am a new creation in Christ (John 3:3–6).

GENERAL RESOURCES

• • •

WHO DOES GOD SAY I AM?

♦ **I am a child of God.**

Yet to all who did receive him, to those who believed in his name, he gave the right to become children of God. (John 1:12)

♦ **I am a branch of the true vine, and a conduit of Christ's life.**

I am the true vine, and my Father is the gardener…I am the vine; you are the branches. If you remain in me and I in you, you will bear much fruit; apart from me you can do nothing. (John 15:1, 5)

♦ **I am a friend of Jesus.**

I no longer call you servants, because a servant does not know his master's business. Instead, I have called you friends, for everything that I learned from my Father I have made known to you. (John 15:15)

♦ **I am justified and redeemed.**

This righteousness is given through faith in Jesus Christ to all who believe. There is no difference between Jew and Gentile, for all have sinned and fall short of the glory of God, and all are justified freely by his grace through the redemption that came by Christ Jesus. (Romans 3:22–24)

♦ **My old self was crucified with Christ, and I am no longer a slave to sin.**

For we know that our old self was crucified with him so that the body ruled by sin might be done away with, that we should no longer be slaves to sin—because anyone who has died has been set free from sin. (Romans 6:6–7)

♦ **God will not condemn me.**

Therefore, there is now no condemnation for those who are in Christ Jesus…(Romans 8:1)

• **I am set free from the law of sin and death.**

For through Christ Jesus the law of the Spirit who give life has set you free from the law of sin and death. (Romans 8:2)

• **As a child of God, I am a fellow heir with Christ.**

Now if we are children, then we are heirs—heirs of God and co-heirs with Christ, if indeed we share in his sufferings in order that we may also share in his glory. (Romans 8:17)

• **Christ accepts me.**

Accept one another, then, just as Christ accepted you, in order to bring praise to God. (Romans 15:7)

• **I am called to be a saint.**

To the church of God in Corinth, to those sanctified in Christ Jesus and called to be his holy people, together with all those everywhere who call on the name of our Lord Jesus Christ—their Lord and ours. (1 Corinthians 1:2; see also Ephesians 1:1; Philippians 1:1; Colossians 1:2)

• **In Christ Jesus, I have wisdom, righteousness, sanctification, and redemption.**

It is because of him that you are in Christ Jesus, who has become for us wisdom from God—that is, our righteousness, holiness and redemption. (1 Corinthians 1:30)

• **My body is the temple of the Holy Spirit, who dwells in me.**

Don't you know that you yourselves are God's temple and that God's Spirit dwells in your midst?…Do you not know that your bodies are temples of the Holy Spirit, who is in you, whom you have received from God? You are not your own; you were bought at a price. Therefore honor God with your bodies. (1 Corinthians 3:16; 6:19–20)

• **I am joined to the Lord and am one in spirit with him.**

But whoever is united with the Lord is one with him in spirit. (1 Corinthians 6:17)

• God leads me in the triumph and knowledge of Christ.

But thanks be to God, who always leads us as captives in Christ's triumphal procession and uses us to spread the aroma of the knowledge of him everywhere. (2 Corinthians 2:14)

• The hardening of my mind has been removed in Christ.

But their minds were made dull, for to this day the same veil remains when the old covenant is read. It has not been removed, because only in Christ is it taken away. (2 Corinthians 3:14)

• I am a new creature in Christ.

Therefore, if anyone is in Christ, the new creation has come; the old has gone, the new is here! (2 Corinthians 5:17)

• I have become the righteousness of God in Christ.

God made him who had no sin to be sin for us, so that in him we might become the righteousness of God. (2 Corinthians 5:21)

• I have been made one with all who are in Christ Jesus.

There is neither Jew nor Gentile, neither slave nor free, nor is there male and female, for you are all one in Christ Jesus. (Galatians 3:28)

• I am no longer a slave but a child and an heir.

So you are no longer a slave, but God's child; and since you are his child, God has made you also an heir. (Galatians 4:7)

• I have been set free in Christ.

It is for freedom that Christ has set us free. Stand firm, then, and do not let yourselves be burdened again by a yoke of slavery. (Galatians 5:1)

• I have been blessed with every spiritual blessing in the heavenly places.

Praise be to the God and Father of our Lord Jesus Christ, who has blessed us in the heavenly realms with every spiritual blessing in Christ. (Ephesians 1:3)

240

- **I am chosen, holy, and blameless before God.**

For he chose us in him before the creation of the world to be holy and blameless in his sight. (Ephesians 1:4)

- **I am redeemed and forgiven by the grace of Christ.**

In him we have redemption through his blood, the forgiveness of sins, in accordance with the riches of God's grace... (Ephesians 1:7)

- **I have been predestined by God to obtain an inheritance.**

To be put into effect when the times reach their fulfillment—to bring unity to all things in heaven and on earth under Christ. In him we were also chosen, having been predestined according to the plan of him who works out everything in conformity with the purpose of his will. (Ephesians 1:10–11)

- **I have been sealed with the Holy Spirit of promise.**

And you also were included in Christ when you heard the message of truth, the gospel of your salvation. When you believed, you were marked in him with a seal, the promised Holy Spirit. (Ephesians 1:13)

- **Because of God's mercy and love, I have been made alive with Christ.**

But because of his great love for us, God, who is rich in mercy, made us alive with Christ even when we were dead in transgressions—it is by grace you have been saved. (Ephesians 2:4–5)

- **I am seated in the heavenly places with Christ.**

And God raised us up with Christ and seated us with him in the heavenly realms in Christ Jesus. (Ephesians 2:6)

- **I am God's workmanship created to produce good works.**

For we are God's handiwork, created in Christ Jesus to do good works, which God prepared in advance for us to do. (Ephesians 2:10)

- **I have been brought near to God by the blood of Christ.**

  But now in Christ Jesus you who once were far away have been brought near by the blood of Christ. (Ephesians 2:13)

- **I am a member of Christ's body and a partaker of his promise.**

  This mystery is that through the gospel the Gentiles are heirs together with Israel, members together of one body, and sharers together in the promise in Christ Jesus…for we are members of his body. (Ephesians 3:6; 5:30)

- **I have boldness and confident access to God through faith in Christ.**

  In him and through faith in him we may approach God with freedom and confidence. (Ephesians 3:12)

- **My new self is righteous and holy.**

  Put on the new self, created to be like God in true righteousness and holiness. (Ephesians 4:24)

- **I was formerly darkness, but now I am light in the Lord.**

  For you were once darkness, but now you are light in the Lord. Live as children of light. (Ephesians 5:8)

- **I am a citizen of heaven.**

  But our citizenship is in heaven. And we eagerly await a Savior from there, the Lord Jesus Christ. (Philippians 3:20)

- **The peace of God guards my heart and mind.**

  And the peace of God, which transcends all understanding, will guard your hearts and your minds in Christ Jesus. (Philippians 4:7)

- **God supplies all my needs.**

  And my God will meet all your needs according to the riches of his glory in Christ Jesus. (Philippians 4:19)

- **I have been made complete in Christ.**

In Christ you have been brought to fullness. He is the head over every power and authority. (Colossians 2:10)

- **I have been raised with Christ.**

Since, then, you have been raised with Christ, set your hearts on things above, where Christ is, seated at the right hand of God. (Colossians 3:1)

- **My life is hidden with Christ in God.**

For you died, and your life is now hidden with Christ in God. (Colossians 3:3)

- **Christ is my life, and I will be revealed with him in glory.**

When Christ, who is your life, appears, then you also will appear with him in glory. (Colossians 3:4)

- **I have been chosen of God, and I am holy and beloved.**

Therefore, as God's chosen people, holy and dearly loved, clothe yourselves with compassion, kindness, humility, gentleness and patience. (Colossians 3:12)

- **God loves me and has chosen me.**

For we know, brothers and sisters loved by God, that he has chosen you. (1 Thessalonians 1:4)

SCRIPTURE MEMORY SUMMARY

Attributes Overview—Matthew 4:19

"Come, follow me," Jesus said, "and I will send you out to fish for people."

Attribute One • Learn to Be With Jesus—Matthew 11:28–30

[28] "Come to me, all you who are weary and burdened, and I will give you rest. [29] Take my yoke upon you and learn from me, for I am gentle and humble in heart, and you will find rest for your souls. [30] For my yoke is easy and my burden is light."

Attribute Two • Learn to Listen—Matthew 7:24–25

[24] "Therefore everyone who hears these words of mine and puts them into practice is like a wise man who built his house on the rock. [25] The rain came down, the streams rose, and the winds blew and beat against that house; yet it did not fall, because it had its foundation on the rock."

Attribute Three • Learn to Heal—Matthew 7:7–8

[7] "Ask and it will be given to you; seek and you will find; knock and the door will be opened to you. [8] For everyone who asks receives; the one who seeks finds; and to the one who knocks, the door will be opened."

Attribute Four • Learn to Influence—Matthew 28:18–20

[18] Then Jesus came to them and said, "All authority in heaven and on earth has been given to me. [19] Therefore go and make disciples of all nations, baptizing them in the name of the Father and of the Son and of the Holy Spirit, [20] and teaching them to obey everything I have commanded you. And surely I am with you always, to the very end of the age."

Attribute Five • Learn to Love—Matthew 22:37–39

[37] Jesus replied: "'Love the Lord your God with all your heart and with all your soul and with all your mind.' [38] This is the first and greatest commandment. [39] And the second is like it: 'Love your neighbor as yourself.'"

Attribute Six • Learn to Pray—Matthew 6:9–13

[9] "This, then, is how you should pray: 'Our Father in heaven, hallowed be your name, [10] your kingdom come, your will be done on earth as it is in heaven. [11] Give us today our daily bread. [12] Forgive us

our debts, as we also have forgiven our debtors. [13] And lead us not into temptation, but deliver us from the evil one.'"

Attribute Seven • Learn to Manage—Matthew 6:33

[33] "But seek first his kingdom and his righteousness, and all these things will be given to you as well."

CHALLENGE MEMORY VERSES

Attribute Overview

Proverbs 3:5–6
[5] Trust in the LORD with all your heart and lean not on your own understanding; [6] in all your ways submit to him, and he will make your paths straight.

Jeremiah 29:11
[11] "For I know the plans I have for you," declares the LORD, "plans to prosper you and not to harm you, plans to give you hope and a future."

Attribute One • Learn to Be With Jesus

John 15:5
[5] "I am the vine; you are the branches. If you remain in me and I in you, you will bear much fruit; apart from me you can do nothing."

Matthew 16:24–25
[24] Then Jesus said to his disciples, "Whoever wants to be my disciple must deny themselves and take up their cross and follow me. For whoever wants to save their life will lose it, but whoever loses their life for me will find it."

Galatians 2:20
[20] I have been crucified with Christ and I no longer live, but Christ lives in me. The life I live in the body, I live by faith in the Son of God, who loved me and gave himself for me.

1 John 1:8–10
[8] If we claim to be without sin, we deceive ourselves and the truth is not in us. [9] If we confess our sins, he is faithful and just and will forgive us our sins and purify us from all unrighteousness. [10] If we claim we have not sinned, we make him out to be a liar and his word is not in us.

Attribute Two • Learn to Listen

John 10:27
27 My sheep listen to my voice; I know them, and they follow me.

2 Timothy 3:16–17
16 All Scripture is God-breathed and is useful for teaching, rebuking, correcting and training in righteousness, 17 so that the servant of God may be thoroughly equipped for every good work.

Psalm 119:11
11 I have hidden your word in my heart that I might not sin against you.

Psalm 119:105
105 Your word is a lamp for my feet and a light on my path.

1 Corinthians 10:13
13 No temptation has overtaken you except what is common to mankind. And God is faithful; he will not let you be tempted beyond what you can bear. But when you are tempted, he will also provide a way out so that you can endure it.

Luke 6:46
46 "Why do you call me, 'Lord, Lord,' and do not do what I say?"

Attribute Three • Learn to Heal

Jeremiah 32:27
27 "I am the LORD, the God of all mankind. Is anything too hard for me?"

2 Corinthians 1:3–4
3 Praise be to the God and Father of our Lord Jesus Christ, the Father of compassion and the God of all comfort, 4 who comforts us in all our troubles, so that we can comfort those in any trouble with the comfort we ourselves receive from God.

Psalm 103:2–5
2 Praise the LORD, O my soul, and forget not all his benefits— 3 who forgives all your sins and heals all your diseases, 4 who redeems your life from the pit and crowns you with love and compassion, 5 who satisfies your desires with good things so that your youth is renewed like the eagle's.

1 Peter 2:24

[24] "He himself bore our sins" in his body on the cross, so that we might die to sins and live for righteousness; "by his wounds you have been healed."

Attribute Four • Learn to Influence

Acts 1:8

[8] "But you will receive power when the Holy Spirit comes on you; and you will be my witnesses in Jerusalem, and in all Judea and Samaria, and to the ends of the earth."

John 3:16–17

[16] "For God so loved the world that he gave his one and only Son, that whoever believes in him shall not perish but have eternal life. [17] For God did not send his Son into the world to condemn the world, but to save the world through him."

Ephesians 2:8–10

[8] For it is by grace you have been saved, through faith—and this is not from yourselves, it is the gift of God— [9] not by works, so that no one can boast. [10] For we are God's handiwork, created in Christ Jesus to do good works, which God prepared in advance for us to do.

Luke 19:10

[10] "For the Son of Man came to seek and to save the lost."

2 Peter 3:9

[9] The Lord is not slow in keeping his promise, as some understand slowness. Instead he is patient with you, not wanting anyone to perish, but everyone to come to repentance.

Mark 10:45

[45] For even the Son of Man did not come to be served, but to serve, and to give his life as a ransom for many."

1 John 5:11–12

[11] And this is the testimony: God has given us eternal life, and this life is in his Son. [12] Whoever has the Son has life; whoever does not have the Son of God does not have life.

Romans 10:14–15

[14] How, then, can they call on the one they have not believed in? And how can they believe in the one of whom they have not heard? And how can they hear without someone preaching to them? [15] And how can

anyone preach unless they are sent? As it is written, "How beautiful are the feet of those who bring good news!"

Attribute Five • Learn to Love

2 Corinthians 5:17

¹⁷ Therefore, if anyone is in Christ, the new creation has come; the old has gone, the new is here!

Psalm 37:4–6

⁴ Take delight in the LORD, and he will give you the desires of your heart. ⁵ Commit your way to the LORD; trust in him and he will do this: ⁶ He will make your righteous reward shine like the dawn, your vindication like the noonday sun.

Philippians 4:4–7

⁴ Rejoice in the Lord always. I will say it again: Rejoice! ⁵ Let your gentleness be evident to all. The Lord is near. ⁶ Do not be anxious about anything, but in every situation, by prayer and petition, with thanksgiving, present your requests to God. ⁷ And the peace of God, which transcends all understanding, will guard your hearts and your minds in Christ Jesus.

Lamentations 3:22–25

²² Because of the LORD's great love we are not consumed, for his compassions never fail. ²³ They are new every morning; great is your faithfulness. ²⁴ I say to myself, "The LORD is my portion; therefore I will wait for him." ²⁵ The LORD is good to those whose hope is in him, to the one who seeks him.

Attribute Six • Learn to Pray

Ephesians 6:18

¹⁸ And pray in the Spirit on all occasions with all kinds of prayers and requests. With this in mind, be alert and always keep on praying for all the Lord's people.

1 Timothy 2:1–2

¹ I urge, then, first of all, that petitions, prayers, intercession and thanksgiving be made for all people— ² for kings and all those in authority, that we may live peaceful and quiet lives in all godliness and holiness.

Jeremiah 33:3

³ 'Call to me and I will answer you and tell you great and unsearchable things you do not know.'

Isaiah 55:8–11

⁸ "For my thoughts are not your thoughts, neither are your ways my ways," declares the LORD. ⁹ "As the heavens are higher than the earth, so are my ways higher than your ways and my thoughts than your thoughts. ¹⁰ As the rain and the snow come down from heaven, and do not return to it without watering the earth and making it bud and flourish, so that it yields seed for the sower and bread for the eater, ¹¹ so is my word that goes out from my mouth: It will not return to me empty, but will accomplish what I desire and achieve the purpose for which I sent it."

John 15:7–8

⁷ If you remain in me and my words remain in you, ask whatever you wish, and it will be done for you. ⁸ This is to my Father's glory, that you bear much fruit, showing yourselves to be my disciples.

Attribute Seven • Learn to Manage

Matthew 6:19–21

¹⁹ "Do not store up for yourselves treasures on earth, where moths and vermin destroy, and where thieves break in and steal. ²⁰ But store up for yourselves treasures in heaven, where moths and vermin do not destroy, and where thieves do not break in and steal. ²¹ For where your treasure is, there your heart will be also."

Proverbs 16:3

³ Commit to the LORD whatever you do, and he will establish your plans.

Proverbs 3:9–10

⁹ Honor the LORD with your wealth, with the firstfruits of all your crops; ¹⁰ then your barns will be filled to overflowing, and your vats will brim over with new wine.

Titus 1:7–9

⁷ Since an overseer manages God's household, he must be blameless—not overbearing, not quick-tempered, not given to drunkenness, not violent, not pursuing dishonest gain. ⁸ Rather, he must be hospitable, one who loves what is good, who is self-controlled, upright, holy and disciplined. ⁹ He must hold firmly to the trustworthy message as it has been taught, so that he can encourage others by sound doctrine and refute those who oppose it.

SELECTED BIBLIOGRAPHY

* Indicates the recommended first book to read on an attribute.

Attribute One • Learn to Be With Jesus

Barton, Ruth Haley. *Sacred Rhythms: Arranging Our Lives for Spiritual Transformation.* InterVarsity, 2006.

Blackaby, Henry, Richard Blackaby, and Claude King. *Experiencing God,* rev. ed. Nashville: Broadman & Holman, 2008.

Bonhoeffer, Dietrich. *Life Together.* New York: Harper and Row, 1976.

———. *The Cost of Discipleship.* Riverside, NJ: MacMillan Publishing, 1967.

Brother Lawrence, *The Practice of the Presence of God.* New York: Doubleday, 1977.

* Foster, Richard. *Celebration of Discipline.* San Francisco: Harper, 1988.

Law, William. *A Serious Call to a Devout and Holy Life.* Philadelphia: Westminster, 1955.

Merton, Thomas. *Contemplative Prayer.* Garden City, NY: Doubleday and Co., 1971.

Murray, Andrew. *Abide in Christ.* New York: Whitaker House, 2002.

Sheldon, Charles. *In His Steps.* Nashville, TN: Broadman, 1935.

Smith, Gordon T. *The Voice of Jesus: Discernment, Prayer, and the Witness of the Spirit.* Downers Grove, IL: InterVarsity, 2003.

Willard, Dallas. *Spirit of the Disciplines.* San Francisco: Harper and Row, 1991 (1990).

Attribute Two • Learn to Listen

Chamber, Oswald. *My Utmost for His Highest.* New York: Mead, 1935.

* Fee, Gordon and Douglas Stuart. *How to Read the Bible for All Its Worth.* Grand Rapids: Zondervan, 2003.

Hendricks, Howard G. and William D. Hendricks, *Living By the Book.* Chicago: Moody, 1991.

Attribute Three • Learn to Heal

Anderson, Neil. *The Bondage Breaker.* Eugene, OR: Harvest House Publishers, 1993.

Baker, John. *Life's Healing Choices: Freedom from Your Hurts, Hang-ups, and Habits.* New York: Howard Books, 2007.

Bosworth, F. F. *Christ the Healer.* Old Tappan, NJ: Fleming, 1973.

Cloud, Henry and John Townsend. *Boundaries.* Grand Rapids: Zondervan, 1992.

* Richards, James. *How to Stop the Pain.* New Kensington, PA: Whitaker House, 2001.

Sande, Ken. *The Peace Maker.* Grand Rapids: Baker, 2004.

Seamands, David A. *Healing for Damaged Emotions.* Colorado Springs: David C. Cook, 1981.

Attribute Four • Learn to Influence

Aldrich, Joe. *Life-Style Evangelism.* Sisters, OR: Multnomah, 2006.

Carnegie, Dale. *How to Win Friends & Influence People.* New York: Pocket Books, 1936.

Cox, Harvey. *Fire from Heaven.* New York: Addison-Wesley, 1995.

Deere, Jack. *Surprised By the Power of the Spirit.* Grand Rapids: Zondervan, 1993.

Egli, Jim and Ben Hoerr. *The I-Factor.* Houston: Touch Publications, 1993.

Fee, Gordon. *God's Empowering Presence.* Peabody, MA: Hendrickson, 1994.

Ford, Leighton. *Good News Is for Sharing.* Elgin, IL: David C. Cook, 1977.

Greenfield, John. *Power from on High.* Muskegon, MI: Dust to Ashes Publications, 1996.

Gumbel, Nicky. *Questions of Life.* Colorado Springs: David C. Cook, 2004.

Hurst, Randy. *The Helper.* Springfield, MO: Gospel Publishing House, 2004.

*Hybels, Bill and Mark Middelberg. *Becoming a Contagious Christian.* Grand Rapids: Eerdmans, 1994.

Kinnaman, David and Gabe Lyons. *UnChristian.* Grand Rapids: Baker, 2007.

Lewis, C. S. *Mere Christianity.* New York: Macmillan, 1960.

Little, Paul. *Know Why You Believe.* Wheaton: Victor Books, 1974.

———. *How to Give Away Your Faith.* Downers Grove, IL: InterVarsity Press, 1988.

McDowell, Josh. *More Than a Carpenter.* Wheaton: Tyndale, 1977.

McLaren, Brian. *Finding Faith.* Grand Rapids: Zondervan, 2007.

———. *More Ready Than You Realize.* Grand Rapids: Zondervan, 2002.

Menzies, William W. and Robert P. Menzies. *Spirit and Power.* Grand Rapids: Zondervan, 2000.

Nouwen, Henri. *In the Name of Jesus.* New York: Crossroads Publishing Company, 1992.

Pippert, Rebecca Manley. *Out of the Salt Shaker and Into the World.* Downers Grove, IL: InterVarsity Press, 1979.

Sherrill, John L. *They Speak with Other Tongues.* New York: Jove, 1964.

Strobel, Lee. *A Case for a Creator.* Grand Rapids: Zondervan, 2004.

———. *A Case For Christ.* Grand Rapids: Zondervan, 1998.

———. *A Case For Faith.* Grand Rapids: Zondervan, 2000.

Wood, George O. *Living in the Spirit.* Springfield, MO: 2009.

Attribute Five • Learn to Love

Crabb, Larry. *Finding God.* Grand Rapids: Zondervan, 1993.

*McGee, Robert. *The Search for Significance.* Houston: Rapha Publishing, 1990.

Mahaney, C. J. *The Cross Centered Life.* Sisters, OR: Multnomah, 2002.

Packer, J. I. *Knowing God.* Downers Grove, IL: InterVarsity Press, 1973.

Attribute Six • Learn to Pray

Bounds, E.M. *A Treasury of Prayer*. Minneapolis: Bethany Fellowship, Inc., 1960.

Eastman, Dick. *The Hour That Changes the World*. Grand Rapids: Baker, 1978.

Foster, Richard J. *Prayer*. San Francisco: Harper, 1992.

Grubb, Norman P. *Rees Howells Intercessor*. Philadelphia: Christian Literature Crusade, 1952.

*Hybels, Bill. *Too Busy Not To Pray*. Downers Grove: InterVarsity Press, 1988.

Murray, Andrew. *With Christ in the School of Prayer*. Philadelphia: H. Altemus, 1895.

Yancey, Philip. *Prayer: Does It Make Any Difference?* Grand Rapids: Zondervan, 2006.

Attribute Seven • Learn to Manage

Carnegie, Dale. *How to Win Friends & Influence People*. New York: Pocket Books, 1936.

Covey, Stephen. *The 7 Habits of Highly Effective People*. New York: Simon & Schuster, 1989.

Duncan, Todd. *Time Traps*. Nashville: Thomas Nelson, 2004.

*MacDonald, Gordon. *Ordering Your Private World*. Nashville: Thomas Nelson, 1984.

Maxwell, John C. *Developing the Leader Within You*. Nashville: Thomas Nelson, 1993.

———. *The Winning Attitude*. Nashville: Thomas Nelson, 1993.

Ramsey, Dave. *Total Money Makeover*. Nashville: Thomas Nelson, 2007.

Smith, Hyrum W. *The 10 Natural Laws of Successful Time and Life Management*. New York: Warner Brothers, 1994.

Swenson, Richard A. *Margin: Restoring Emotional, Physical, Financial, and Time Reserves to Overloaded Lives*. Colorado Springs: NavPress, 1992.

———. *The Overload Syndrome: Learning to Live Within Your Limits*. Colorado Springs: NavPress, 1998.

Winston, Stephanie. *Getting Organized*. New York: Grand Central Publishing, 2006.

www.mypyramid.gov

SPIRITUAL COACHING
RESOURCES

• • •

What is a Spiritual Coach?

A spiritual coach is one who comes alongside another person to help him or her become an authentic follower of Christ.

- **Coming Alongside**
  - You are on the journey with the person. You are not over the person.
  - Assume an attitude of humility. We are all learning to follow Jesus.
- **Helping**
  - You are there to help.
  - You won't have all the answers.
  - The focus is on the person being coached and not the coach.
- **Authentic Follower of Christ**
  - The goal is that the other person will be an authentic follower of Jesus.
  - The goal is not the completion of material. It is growing in the seven attributes of the follower of Jesus.

What is the Role of a Spiritual Coach?

- To help the person continue to move along the path to following Christ

  Hebrews 10:24, ²⁴"And let us consider how we may spur one another on toward love and good deeds."

- To gently challenge a person to become an authentic follower of Jesus

  Proverbs 27:17, ¹⁷"As iron sharpens iron, so one person sharpens another."

What is the Process of Spiritual Coaching?[1]

* **Relate**—establish coaching relationship and agenda
* **Reflect**—discover and explore key issues
* **Refocus**—determine priorities and action steps
* **Resource**—provide support and encouragement
* **Review**—evaluate, celebrate, and revise plans

What Types of Questions Will I Ask as a Spiritual Coach?

* **Relate**
  + How are you doing?
  + How was your week?

* **Reflect**
  + What stood out to you this week in your reading?
  + What obstacles are you facing?

* **Refocus**
  + What would you like to do?
  + What are some possible ways to get there?

* **Resource**
  + What resources do you have?
  + What resources are you missing?
  + Would you like some accountability around that?

* **Review**
  + What's working?
  + What's not working?
  + What needs to change?

GETTING STARTED COACHING SESSION

1. Introduce yourself if you don't know the person.

2. Turn to the "Getting Started" page and emphasize the following:

   a. Congratulate them—choosing to follow Jesus is the most important decision of their life.

   b. Explain the importance of coming to Christ, hearing his words, and putting them into practice (doing).

   c. Explain the importance of getting involved in a small group.

   d. Explain that you are their spiritual coach. Let them know if, for any reason, they would rather have a different coach, that will be fine with you. You will not be offended. Getting a coach with whom you have good chemistry is important.

   e. Talk about the importance of setting aside about fifteen minutes a day for time with God. Ask them when that will work best. (See the fill in for this.) Have them write it in the book.

   f. Encourage them to write in their book. It will help them apply more to their life.

   g. Make sure the person has a Bible in a modern translation (NIV, TNIV, NLT).

   h. Show them how to do the Scripture memory— drop a word.

      1. Encourage them to pray before they start.
      2. Remind them that the key is reviewing daily.
      3. Tell them you will quiz them when you get together.

3. Review the Seven Attributes from the Table of Contents.

    a. Encourage them to read one a day.

    b. Show them how each of the seven attributes has a chapter and steps all its own.

4. Ask him or her if they have any questions.

5. Ask how you can pray for them.

    a. You may want to write this down and pray for them during the week.

    b. Take the person by the hand (for men the hand shake posture is non-threatening).

    c. Pray that God will bless this person as he or she takes the next steps as a follower of Christ.

6. Exchange phone numbers and e-mail addresses.

7. Set a time for the next meeting(s).

    a. It is best to get a weekly time of about an hour that works for both of you.

    b. Try to schedule out for one or two months if possible.

ATTRIBUTE OVERVIEW COACHING SESSION

Coaches' Note: The Attribute Overview Coaching Session will probably take two to three sessions. Let the person set the pace.

Relate

- How was your week?
  - ⇥ Share briefly about your week if it seems appropriate.
  - ⇥ Express what an honor it is to be able to walk alongside them on their journey as a follower of Christ.
  - ⇥ Explain your role as a spiritual coach—to come alongside and help him or her become an authentic follower of Christ.

- Get to know the person
  - ⇥ Where were you born and raised?
  - ⇥ Tell me a little bit about your family (parents, spouse, children).
  - ⇥ What is your work?

- Share your faith journey.
  - ⇥ As we start on this journey together, it might be helpful for you to know a little bit about my faith journey.
  - ⇥ ***Important:*** It is very important that they hear how Jesus changed your life. This should be a 5–10 minute testimony maximum.

- Tell me about your faith journey.

- How did you decide to make a commitment to Christ?
  - ⇥ Be a good listener.
  - ⇥ Express appropriate emotion but don't side track the conversation.

258

→ Summarize what you hear them saying.

→ Be sensitive to the leading the Holy Spirit.

→ Don't push if they decide to say things vaguely.

Reflect

• How did it go this week in your reading?

• Were you able to find a small group that worked for you?

• How did it go with your 5–15 minutes each day with the Lord?

• Were you able to memorize Matthew 4:19?

→ "Come, follow me," Jesus said, "and I will send you out to fish for people." Matthew 4:19

• Which of the attributes stood out to you the most?

Refocus

Attribute Two • Learn to Listen talked about repentance.

• Was that an encouraging section for you?

• Do you feel comfortable sharing with me some things from which you are repenting?

• What would you like to do about those things?

Resource

• Would you like me to ask you about this next week?

Attribute Three • Learn to Heal

• Is there anything about which I can pray for healing for you?

Attribute Six • Learn to Pray

• Do you think the Lord spoke to you in some way this week?

Refocus

Attribute Seven • Learn to Manage

- What are some places or areas of your life in which you need to invest so that your heart goes where you want it to go?

- What are you going to invest in for each of these areas?

Resource

- Would you like me to ask you about this next week?

Prayer

- How can I pray for you today?
  - Write down their prayer requests on a Prayer Request List in the back of this book. Be sure to write the date it was answered as well.
  - Take them by the hand (for men the hand shake posture is not threatening).
  - Pray for what they asked and that God would bless them as they take the next steps as a follower of Christ.

Review

- Is this helping you in your walk with Jesus?

Set the date and time for the next meeting

- Does this time work for you?
  - Set a day and time for the next meeting(s).
  - Schedule out for 1–2 months if possible.

ATTRIBUTE ONE · LEARN TO BE WITH JESUS COACHING SESSION

Relate

- How are things going?

Review

- Were you able to find a small group that worked for you?

- How did it go with your 5–15 minutes each day with the Lord?

- Do you still remember Matthew 4:19?
  - "Come, follow me," Jesus said, "and I will send you out to fish for people." Matthew 4:19

- Can you recite Matthew 11:28–30?
  - [28] "Come to me, all you who are weary and burdened, and I will give you rest. [29] Take my yoke upon you and learn from me, for I am gentle and humble in heart, and you will find rest for your souls. [30] For my yoke is easy and my burden is light." Matthew 11:28–30

Reflect

- What stood out to you this week in your reading?

- Step 1—Were you able to download any songs from iTunes? Do you need help doing that?

- How is your Bible reading going?

- What kinds of things stood out to you as you read?

Refocus

- Did you make any decisions to do something as a result of what stood out to you?

Resource

♦ Do you need any support to help you with your decisions?

Coaches' Note: See the "How to Develop a Schedule" resource in the Resource section if the person needs help with his or her schedule.

Review

♦ Did anything confuse you this week as you read?

Prayer

♦ How can I pray for you this week?
  → Turn to the prayer list you started for this person.
  → Ask if God has answered their requests from the previous week.
  → Take them by the hand (for men the hand shake posture is not threatening).
  → Pray for what they asked and that God would bless them as they take the next steps as a follower of Christ.

Set the date and time for the next meeting

♦ Schedule out for 1–2 months if possible.

ATTRIBUTE TWO · LEARN TO LISTEN COACHING SESSION

Relate

- What was the highlight of your week?

Review

- How did it go this week with your time with God?

- What challenges did have in spending time with God?

- Were you able to find a small group that worked for you?

- How is it going with Matthew 4:19?
    - "Come, follow me," Jesus said, "and I will send you out to fish for people." Matthew 4:19

- How about Matthew 11:28–30?
    - [28] "Come to me, all you who are weary and burdened, and I will give you rest. [29] Take my yoke upon you and learn from me, for I am gentle and humble in heart, and you will find rest for your souls. [30] For my yoke is easy and my burden is light." Matthew 11:28–30

- How is Matthew 7:24–25 coming?
    - [24] "Therefore everyone who hears these words of mine and puts them into practice is like a wise man who built his house on the rock. [25] The rain came down, the streams rose, and the winds blew and beat against that house; yet it did not fall, because it had its foundation on the rock." Matthew 7:24–25

Reflect

- What stood out to you this week in your reading?

Refocus

- Have you thought about how you are going to incorporate Bible reading into your life?
- Do you have specific questions about God for which you could use an answer?
  - *Coaches' Note:* Listen but don't give answers if you don't have them.
- Do you have some things you need to adjust so you can be more productive for God?
- What are some obstacles you face in doing that?

Resource

- What do you need to make that happen?
- Would you like some accountability around that?
- What would accountability look like for you?

Prayer

- How can I pray for you this week?
  - Turn to the prayer list you started for this person.
  - Ask if God has answered their requests from the previous week.
  - Take them by the hand (for men the hand shake posture is not threatening).
  - Pray for what they asked and that God would bless them as they take the next steps as a follower of Christ.

Set the date and time for the next meeting

- Schedule out for 1–2 months if possible.

ATTRIBUTE THREE · LEARN TO HEAL COACHING SESSION

Relate

- How is your week going?

Review

- What's working? Not working? Missing? Confused?

Reflect

- What stood out to you from the reading this week?

Refocus

- In what area(s) of your life would you like healing?
  Coaches' Note: Take time to pray right now for healing.

Resource

- What could you do to promote healing in your life?
  Coaches' Note: The person should know they can do the following:
    - Ask God to heal them
    - See a doctor if it is something medical
    - Learn about a helpful healing process (Grief, Conflict Resolution, Recovery)
- What resources do you need to find healing?

Prayer

- How can I pray for you this week?
    - Turn to the prayer list you started for this person.
    - Ask if God has answered their requests from the previous week.

- Does anyone around you need healing?
    - Take them by the hand (for men the hand shake posture is not threatening).
    - Pray for what they asked and that God would

bless them as they take the next steps as a follower of Christ.

Set the date and time for the next meeting

• Schedule out for 1–2 months if possible.

ATTRIBUTE FOUR · LEARN TO INFLUENCE COACHING SESSION

Relate
- What's going on in your life this week?

Review
- How is your follow process going?

Reflect
- Did you have a chance to fill out the Evangelism Styles Questionnaire? What was your style?
- Did you make out your prayer list? Did you begin to pray? Did anything happen?
- Did you enjoy writing out your story?
- What did you think about the discussion about the Baptism in the Holy Spirit? Is that something you have experienced? Would like to experience? If yes, encourage them to draw near to Jesus, to wait for the Holy Spirit to come upon them, and to yield to the Spirit's promptings.

Refocus
- In what ways would you like to grow as a result of what you learned this week?

Resource
- What do you need to make that happen?
- How can I support you in that?

Prayer
- How can I pray for you this week?
  - Turn to the prayer list you started for this person.
  - Ask if they would like you to pray for them to receive the Baptism in the Holy Spirit.
  - Pray for what they asked and that God would bless them as they take the next steps as a follower of Christ.

Set the date and time for the next meeting.

ATTRIBUTE FIVE · LEARN TO LOVE COACHING SESSION

Relate

+ What's new in your life this week?

Review

+ Were you able to pray for people on your influence list this week?

+ Did anything unusual happen with any of those relationships?

Reflect

+ Did you take the assessments this week before you worked on each step?

+ Were you low on any of the assessments? Did you agree with the summary?

Refocus

+ What would you like to do as a result of what you learned in Attribute Five?

+ What are some possible ways of doing that?

Resource

+ What resources do you have to make that change?

+ Do you see any obstacles to making that change?

+ Would you like some accountability around that?

+ What would that look like for you?

Prayer

+ How can I pray for you this week?
    + Turn to the prayer list you started for this person.
    + Ask if God has answered their requests from the previous week.

- Pray for what they asked and that God would bless them as they take the next steps as a follower of Christ.

Set the date and time for the next meeting

ATTRIBUTE SIX · LEARN TO PRAY COACHING SESSION

Relate

- What was the highlight of your week?

Review

- How did it go with your thought process this week? (loving God, identifying any lies, replacing the lies with the truth)

- Do you feel like you made some progress?

Reflect

- What stood out to you as you worked through this attribute?

- On Step 2, there was a discussion about areas that we have difficulty giving up control. Did you have any areas you would like to discuss?

- On Step 3, there was a discussion about food. How are you with food?

- What did you think about the process for "Praying Through Pain" on Step 4? Do you have any areas you prayed through or would like to pray through that you want to talk about?

- Did you have any trouble identifying the lie?

- On Step 5, there was a discussion about "praying in the Spirit." Do you have any experience with praying in a prayer language? Is that something you would like to talk about?

Refocus

- What would you like to do as a result of what you read and learned this week?

Resource

- What resources do you need to make that happen?

Prayer

- How can I pray for you this week?
  - Turn to the prayer list you started for this person.
  - Ask if God has answered their requests from the previous week.
  - Pray for what they asked and that God would bless them as they take the next steps as a follower of Christ.

Set the date and time for the next meeting

ATTRIBUTE SEVEN · LEARN TO MANAGE COACHING SESSION

Relate
- How are you doing?

Review
- How is your prayer life coming?
- Have you been able to keep your quiet time consistent this week?
- Did you learn anything in your prayer life this week?

Reflect
- How did it go with the Learn to Manage attribute?
- Are there any key areas that stood out to you?

Refocus
- Did you identify any steps you would like to take with putting God first in your finances?
- How about with your body?
- How is your time management?

Resource
- Is that something with which you would like some support?
- What do you need to get where you want to go in these areas?

Prayer
- How can I pray for you this week?
  - Turn to the prayer list you started for this person.
  - Ask if God has answered their requests from the previous week.
  - Pray for what they asked and that God would bless them as they take the next steps as a follower of Christ.

Set the date and time for the next meeting

COACHING CERTIFICATION QUESTIONS

Learn to Be With Jesus
- How is your faithfulness at church on Sunday morning?
- What is your involvement in a small group?
- Describe your quiet time.

Learn to Listen
- How is your Bible reading going?
- Describe a time recently when you applied God's Word to your life.

Learn to Heal
- Where do you currently need healing?
- Tell about someone for whom you prayed for healing.

Learn to Influence
- Who are some people who are on your prayer list who you pray for regularly to find Christ?
- How are you using your primary mode of evangelism to influence people to follow Jesus?
- How are you influencing your family to follow Jesus?
- How are you influencing people at work to be interested in getting to know more about Jesus?
- Would you tell me your 3 minute testimony?
- How have you incorporated the habit of listening more than you talk as a way to influence others?

Learn to Love
- Describe how learning about God's love and acceptance affects how you love and accept others.
- Describe the last time you felt anxious. How did you handle it?

Learn to Pray

- Describe your prayer life.
- What people or situations are you regularly bringing to God?
- How are you with forgiving others?
- Describe the last time you remembered enjoying worship to God.

Learn to Manage

- How are you managing your body? (sleep, eating, exercise, etc.)
- Describe any unhealthy habits you have (eating, drinking, smoking, drugs, pornography).
- How are you managing your spiritual gifts?
- How are you managing your words?
- How are you managing your finances? (debt, living within your means, giving)
- Do you seek God first in your finances? How so?
- How are you with managing your time?

Coaching

- Who are you planning to coach?

NOTES

Attribute Three • Overview

1. There was nothing that Jesus could not heal. Jesus healed diseases and sicknesses. He also set people free who were dominated by forces of evil.

Attribute Four • Overview

1. Rick Warren, *The Purpose-Driven Life* (Grand Rapids: Zondervan, 2002), 17.

Attribute Five • Overview

1. See Attribute Six–Step 4, "Learn to Pray Through Pain."

Attribute One • Step Three

1. Some find once they become followers of Jesus, they are very hungry to read God's Word. If you are up for the challenge, you can read through the entire Bible in one year by reading about twenty minutes per day. We recommend a YouVersion reading plan (www.youversion.com/reading-plans/all), or check out www.unboundbible.blogspot.com for a yearly Bible reading plan that some of the Spring Valley Community Church family use.

Attribute Two • Step One

1. Haddon Robinson, *What Jesus Said About Successful Living* (Grand Rapids: Discovery House Publishers, 1991), 28.

2. Ibid.

Attribute Two • Step Four

1. If you found Deuteronomy 6:16, you are correct.

Attribute Three • Step One

1. http://www.time.com/time/magazine/article/0,9171,982784-1,00.html.

Attribute Three • Step Five

1. We recommend *When God Doesn't Make Sense* (Wheaton: Tyndale House Publishers, 1997) by James Dobson and *Where Is God When It Hurts* (Grand Rapids: Zondervan, 1990) by Philip Yancey.

Attribute Four • Introduction

1. Unfortunately different groups have polarized about speaking in tongues. Some make "speaking in tongues" the point of the baptism in the Holy Spirit. A simple reading of Acts 1:8 indicates otherwise. Speaking in tongues was the normal part of that experience but not the emphasis. The repetition of the

experience throughout the New Testament (Acts 10, 19; 1 Corinthians 12–14) indicates it was a normal part of the early church and was the expected and normal experience. The purpose of the empowerment of the Spirit is to enable people to effectively witness for Christ. Others argue the experience is not valid for the Christian today, is not expected, and should be avoided. A plain reading of Scripture indicates that empowerment for witnessing was the focus of the experience. The polarization in the church about the issue of speaking in tongues does not honor Jesus. Speaking in tongues is neither a spiritual badge to be worn with pride nor an experience that should be avoided. It is a blessing and a by-product of the empowerment of the Holy Spirit.

Attribute Four • Step One

1. Win and Charles Arn surveyed 14,000 people nationwide to ask them, "What or who was responsible for your coming to Christ?" At least 75 percent of respondents in every context said a friend or a family member was the most significant influence.

2. http://www.barna.org/barna-update/article/5-barna-update/196-evangelism-is-most-effective-among-kids.

3. 80 percent of the people surveyed by Thom Rainer indicated that they would attend a church if they were asked (*The UnChurched Next Door,* Grand Rapids: Zondervan, 2008), 32.

Attribute Five • Introduction

1. Robert McGee, *The Search for Significance* (Houston: Rapha Publishing, 1985).

2. Ibid, 100.

Attribute Five • Step Two

1. Gary L. McIntosh and Samuel D. Rima, *Overcoming the Dark Side of Leadership: The Paradox of Personal Dysfunction* (Grand Rapids: Baker Books, 1998).

Attribute Five • Step Three

1. Robert S. McGee, *The Search for Significance*, 84.

2. Ibid., 85.

Attribute Five • Step Four

1. Robert McGee, *The Search for Significance*, 108-110.

Attribute Six • Introduction

1. The address of Maralyn's blog is http://www.maralynsupdates.blogspot.com.

Attribute Six • Step Two

1. Tim Hughes. "Here I am to Worship" (Thankyou Music. Admin. by EMI Christian Music Publishing, 2000).

2. Stuart Townend. "How Deep the Father's Love for Us" (Admin. by EMI Christian Music Publishing, 1995).

3. Reuben Morgan. "I Give You My Heart" (Admin. by Integrity's Hosanna! Music, 1995).

4. Laura Story. "Indescribable" (Worshiptogether.com songs. Sixsteps Music. Gleaning Publishing. Admin. by EMI Christian Music Publishing, 2004).

5. Jeremy Riddle. "More Than a Friend" (Mercy/Vineyard Publishing. Admin. by Music Services, 2002).

Attribute Six • Step Four

1. This is similar to a process I (Daniel) heard Dr. Richard Dobbins teach in 1994 at Stone Church in Toronto, ON. I also heard Bill Gothard teach something similar about that same time.

2. There are more than sixty lament psalms. There are individual laments (e.g. 3, 22, 31, 42, 57, 69, 71, 120, 139, and 142) and corporate laments (e.g. 12, 44, 80, 94, and 137). The lament usually exhibits the following pattern: Address the LORD; Complain; statement of Trust in the LORD; expectation of Deliverance; Assurance of the LORD's victory; and Praise for the LORD (Gordon Fee and Douglas Stewart, *How to Read the Bible for All Its Worth* [Grand Rapids: Zondervan, 2003]).

Attribute Seven • Step One

1. Walter F. Arndt and F. Wilbur Gingrich, *A Greek-English Lexicon of the New Testament* (Chicago: The University of Chicago Press, 1979), 475.

2. I (Daniel) am not sure to whom this quote belongs. It has been attributed to Ralph Waldo Emerson (1803–1882), Charles Reade (1814–1884), and a Buddist Proverb.

Attribute Seven • Step Two

1. This was discussed in Overview Attribute Seven.

Attribute Seven • Step Five

1. I (Daniel) first heard about this story in Richard Swenson's book, *The Overload Syndrome* (Colorado Springs: NavPress, 1998), 23–24.

2. Proverbs 6:6–11, 10:26, 13:4, 15:19, 19:24, 20:4, 21:25–26, 22:13, 24:30–34, 26:13–16.

Resources • Attribute Three

1. David H. Olson, *Prepare/Enrich Counselor's Manual* (Minneapolis: Life Innovations, Inc, 1982, 1986, 1996), 63–64.

2. Elisabeth Kubler-Ross and David Kessler, *On Grief and Grieving: Finding the Meaning of Grief Through the Five Stages of Loss* (New York: Scribner, 2005).

3. http://www.celebraterecovery.com.

Resources • Attribute Four

1. Taken from ***Becoming a Contagious Christian Participant's Guide*** by LEE P. STROBEL; BILL HYBELS; MARK MITTELBERG. Copyright © 1995, 2007 by Willow Creek Community Church. Used by permission of Zondervan. WWW.ZONDERVAN.COM.

Resources • Attribute Five

1. Robert S. McGee, *The Search for Significance* (Houston: Rapha Publishing, 1985), 46–47. Used by permission.

2. Ibid., 66–67.

3. Ibid., 90–91.

4. Ibid., 105–106.

5. Ibid., 40–41.

Spiritual Coaching Resources

1. The coaching model adopted in this resource, particularly the 5Rs of coaching, comes from *Coaching 101* by Robert E. Logan, Sherilyn Carlton, and Tara Miller (ChurchSmart Resources, 2003). Used by permission.

SCRIPTURE REFERENCE INDEX

TOPICAL INDEX

PRAYER REQUEST LIST

Request   **Date**   **Date Answered**

PRAYER REQUEST LIST

Request	Date	Date Answered

PRAYER REQUEST LIST

Request	Date	Date Answered

CPSIA information can be obtained
at www.ICGtesting.com
Printed in the USA
BVHW090919210620
581974BV00006B/731